BOOK 1 OF THE
ADULT LEARNER SERIES

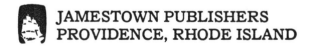

Murder by Radio

JUDITH ANDREWS GREEN
SUPERVISOR,
READING CLINIC
UNIVERSITY OF MAINE,
FARMINGTON

JAMESTOWN PUBLISHERS
PROVIDENCE, RHODE ISLAND

Cover Design by Stephen R. Anthony
Cover Illustration and
Story Illustrations by David Ireland

Printed in the United States   KI

86 87 88 9 8 7 6 5 4 3

ISBN 0-89061-152-5

Titles in This Series

No. 200, Murder by Radio
No. 201, The Man Who Stopped Time
No. 202, The Man with the Scar
No. 203, Dr. Valdez
No. 204, The Secret of Room 401
No. 205, A City for Ransom
No. 206, Nightmare Snow
No. 207, Peril on the Road
No. 208, Killer in a Trance?

To Maggie Scholl
with thanks for all her help

ACKNOWLEDGMENTS

To all my students whose suggestions and criticisms were so helpful, I am most grateful. My thanks to the Jamestown editorial staff for help in preparing and writing the exercises which appear in this book.

TO THE READER

Tom Ladd found his uncle murdered. Tom had to find out who had killed him . . . and why!

And then he found out that someone was trying to kill *him!*

As you read these stories, watch everyone you meet. See if you can tell who the murderer is.

Before each story begins, there are words for you to look at and learn. These words are in sentences so you can see how they will be used in the story. After each story there are questions for you to answer. These questions will give you an idea of how well you are reading.

Another part that comes with each story is called Language Skills. These parts are lessons which will help you to read, write and spell better.

The last two parts with every story deal with Life Skills. These are things you need to know about and know how to do to get along in life.

The answers to all the questions and exercises are in the back of the book. This lets you check your answers to see if they are right.

We hope you will like reading *Murder by Radio* and learning all of the things this book teaches.

CONTENTS

How to Use This Book

1. Learn the Preview Words

Say the words in the box. Then read the sentences. Try to learn the words. See if you know what each sentence means.

2. Read the Story

As you read, try to follow the story and what the people in it are doing. See if you can find out who the murderer is.

3. Answer: Comprehension Questions

Put an *x* in the box next to the best answer to each question. Read all ten questions first and answer the easy ones. Then go back and answer the hard ones.

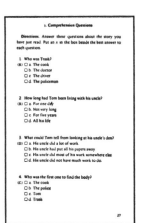

4. Correct Your Answers

Use the Answer Key on page 167. If your answer is wrong, circle that box and put an *x* in the right box.

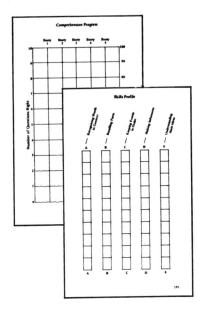

5. Fill in the Graphs

Fill in the graph on page 189 to show your comprehension score. Use the graph on page 191 to chart your skills.

6. Read: Language Skills

This comes after the questions. Read the pages and do the exercises. Use the Answer Key on page 169 to correct the exercises.

7. Read: Understanding Life Skills

Read these pages and follow the step-by-step lessons. Use the Answer Key on page 179 to check your answers.

8. Practice: Applying Life Skills

Read the instructions and do the Life Skills exercise. Take your time. Do the work carefully. Try to remember what you just read about understanding life skills. Use the Answer Key on page 181 to correct the exercise.

9. Read the Story Again

Go back to the story and read it once more. This time, as you read, try to feel all the interest and excitement the writer has built in.

Then, go on to the Preview Words for the next story.

1. Preview Words

Study the words in the box. Then read the sentences below with your teacher. Look carefully at the words with lines under them.

again	friends	lawyer	shook
anything	funeral	never	someone
breakfast	happened	nothing	suddenly
dead	heart	policeman	thought
does	knew	right	very

1. Someone was screaming.
2. There it was again.
3. Mr. Ladd! Your uncle is dead!
4. Tom had never been in it.
5. Tom had not lived with his uncle very long.
6. "What happened?" Tom asked.
7. I thought I would make him a cup of tea.
8. It must have been his heart.
9. Suddenly he got down next to him.
10. "Look," he said. "He had lost a tooth. Right in front."
11. I never knew that he had lost a tooth.
12. One policeman came up to Tom.
13. No, we could not find anything.
14. The policeman shook his head.
15. There was nothing for Tom to do, so he went to bed.
16. As long as you are up, I should make you some breakfast.
17. He called his uncle's lawyer.
18. Would you like me to take care of your uncle's funeral?
19. Will you call his friends?
20. He does not live here now.

1. What Happened?

CHAPTER ONE

Someone was screaming.

Tom Ladd woke up fast. He sat up in bed. What was it? What was up?

There it was again. Someone *was* screaming.

Who was it? What was going on?

Tom got out of bed fast. He looked for the light. He fell over a chair. What was going on?

Just then, someone ran down the hall. "Mr. Ladd! Mr. Ladd!" someone shouted.

Tom got up and ran to the door. "What is it?" he shouted. "What is going on?"

A man ran in. It was Trask, the man who drove his uncle's car, a big Rolls.

"Mr. Ladd! Your uncle is dead!" Trask said.

"Dead! How? He . . ."

"Come with me!" Trask said. They ran down the hall and down the stairs.

"In there!" Trask said. "His body is in there!"

Tom went into his uncle's den. This was the room where his uncle worked. Tom had never been in it.

Tom had not lived with his uncle very long. He was living with his uncle while he looked for a new job. He did not see much of his uncle. So he did not know what his uncle was working on. His uncle never talked about it. And Tom had never asked him.

Now Tom went into the den. He looked around. The room was full of papers and books. There were piles of books all around the room. The table was full of papers, and there were more papers on the floor. The room was so full of things that Tom did not see his uncle at first.

Then he saw him.

His uncle was lying on the floor by the table. He still had some papers in his hand. His mouth was open. His chair was tipped over on its side.

The cook was in the room, too. She was looking down at the body and crying.

"What happened?" Tom asked.

"Oh, Mr. Ladd! Your poor uncle! Your uncle is dead!" the cook said.

"But what happened?" Tom asked again.

"Well, I woke up in the night," the cook said. "I got up and I saw that his light was still on. So I thought I would make him a cup of tea. He liked a cup of tea when he was working late. He ... he ... he ..." The cook was crying again.

"There, there," Tom said. "Then what happened?"

"So I made him a cup of tea. But when I came in, he was lying on the floor. I ran to him, but he was ... he was dead."

"What did you do then?" Tom asked.

"Well, I screamed," the cook said. "Then Trask came in, and he ran to get you."

"Was my uncle ever sick before?" Tom asked.

"No, he was never sick," the cook said. "But it must have been his heart. Look at him. Look at his mouth. He must have tried to call for help."

Tom went over to the body. "Poor Uncle Ned," he said, "I wish that I had gotten to know you more."

He looked down at his uncle. Suddenly he got down next to him. He looked into his mouth.

"Look," he said. "He had lost a tooth. Right in front."

18

"Had he? That is funny," the cook said. "I never knew that he had lost a tooth."

"How about you, Trask?" Tom asked. "Did you know that?"

"Um, no ... He could have ... I never looked," Trask said.

Tom got up. "Yes. Well. Trask, will you make a phone call?"

"Do you want me to call a doctor?" Trask asked.

"No," Tom said. "I want you to call the police."

"The police!" said the cook.

"Yes. There is something funny going on here. I think that my uncle has been murdered."

CHAPTER TWO

The police came quickly. They looked at the body. They looked at the room. They talked to Tom and the cook and Trask.

At last they were done. One policeman came up to Tom. "Well, Mr. Ladd," he said, "everything seems to be all right. We do not think that your uncle was murdered."

"No?" Tom asked.

"No, we could not find anything. The room is OK. His papers are all right. There was no fight. If he had been murdered, there would have been a fight."

"But look at his face! Look at his mouth!" Tom said.

"OK. OK. So his mouth is open. The cook was right. He tried to call for help."

"But . . . but . . . *Look* at his face! He does not look as if he were calling for help. He looks . . . well, he looks funny." Tom stopped. The policeman just looked at him.

"What about the tooth?" Tom asked.

"What about it? That tooth did not just fall out. It has been gone for a long time. Mr. Trask said that he thinks he knew that it was gone. You just never looked. How long have you lived here?"

"I have lived here for three weeks," Tom said.

"You see? You just never looked. Your uncle spent most of his time in here. You did not know him that well. You just never looked." The policeman shook his head. "No, Mr. Ladd, he was an old man. It was his heart. He jumped up fast. Look at his chair. There it is, on its side. He tried to call for help. Then he fell. It was his heart."

"But . . ."

"No, Mr. Ladd, there is just nothing here to make us think he was murdered."

Tom tried and tried to talk to the other policemen, but they said the same thing. "It was his heart, Mr. Ladd. He was an old man."

At last they left. Someone came and took away the body. It was very late.

There was nothing for Tom to do, so he went to bed. He tried to go to sleep, but he could not. He could not stop thinking about his uncle.

"I wish that I had got to know him more," he thought. "What was he working on? Was that it? Would someone kill him for it?

"Who would kill an old man like that? The police must have been right. The room was all right. There had been no fight. It must have been his heart.

"But his face! Why did it look like that? It just did not look right."

Tom tried and tried to sleep. At last he sat up in bed.

"What was he working on? I can find *that* out!" he said to himself. He got up. He went quietly down the hall and down the stairs. He went into his uncle's den.

He turned on the light. The den was just as they had left it. Papers were piled up on the table and the floor. Books were piled up all around the room. Where would he start?

Tom went over to the table. He looked at the pile of papers. He picked up the paper on top. It was full of letters and numbers. They did not seem to mean anything.

Tom looked at the next paper, and the next. They were all full of letters and numbers. But what did they mean?

Suddenly, Tom felt someone watching him. He looked up fast.

Trask was standing by the door. When Tom looked at him, he said, "I saw the light on."

"Yes," Tom said.

"I . . . um . . . I just thought I would see what was up," Trask said. "What are you looking for?"

"I could not sleep," Tom said. "So I thought I would look at my uncle's papers. I want to know what he was working on."

"He did not want anyone to know," Trask said.

"I know. But he was my uncle. I am all he had. So all the papers and books are mine now."

"Well, all right." Just as suddenly as he had come, Trask was gone.

"What was that all about?" Tom asked himself. "What is he up to? I think I will have to watch him."

CHAPTER THREE

Soon the cook came in. "You poor thing," she said to Tom. "Have you been up all night, too?"

"Yes," Tom said. "I could not sleep."

"I know. I could not help thinking about your poor uncle. What a good man he was. And now he is gone." She looked as if she were going to cry again.

"So I thought I would look at his papers," Tom said quickly. "I want to find out what he was working on."

"Oh, that is nice," said the cook. "Did you find out?"

"No. The papers do not mean very much to me."

"He was such a smart man," the cook said. "Well, as long as you are up, I should make you some breakfast."

"Breakfast! Is it that late?" Tom asked. "It looks like I have lost a night's sleep! Yes, I think I will have some breakfast now."

The cook went out, and Tom went on looking at the papers. All those letters and numbers. What did they mean?

He looked at the books. They were not much better. By the time the cook came in to call him for breakfast, he wanted to give up.

After breakfast, Tom did not go back to his uncle's den. He had a call to make.

He called his uncle's lawyer. "My uncle died last night," he told him. "The police said that it was a heart attack."

"That is too bad," the lawyer said. "It is very sad that he should die just now. I know that he was working on something very big."

"Do you know what it was?" Tom asked.

"No, he never told me. He just said that it would be very big. Now, would you like me to take care of your uncle's funeral? Would you like me to get everything set?" the lawyer asked.

"Yes!" Tom said. "That would be very good of you. I . . . I have never done anything like that before."

"All right, then. I will take care of everything. Now, will you call his friends?" the lawyer asked.

"His friends! Do you know who they are?" Tom asked.

"No, I do not. But if you look through his papers, you should find their names."

"His papers . . ." Tom said sadly. "Yes, I will try."

"Good-bye," the lawyer said. "Thank you for calling me."

"Good-bye," Tom said.

Tom went back to his uncle's den. He looked through all the papers and books again. He looked and looked for a book that would have the names and phone numbers of his uncle's friends.

As he looked, he tried to think. "Was he murdered?" he asked himself. "Or was it his heart? What about his face? What about Trask?" It all went around and around in his head.

"How will I find out what he was working on?" he asked himself. "What do all these papers mean?"

Then he thought of something. His friends! Some of them might know what his uncle was working on. He could ask them. But could he find out who they were?

At last he found a little book. He looked at it. There was not much in it. But there were some names in it. And there were some phone numbers. Now he would find out what he wanted to know.

Tom felt good as he called the first number. Now he would find out what was going on. His uncle's friends would tell him.

But the first number was not a friend of his uncle. It was a store.

Tom called the next number. But when he asked for the name, a woman said, "He does not live here now."

Tom felt sad. "This is not going to work," he thought. "Oh, well, I will try again."

He called the next number. It was a man. "Is this Mr. Day?" Tom asked.

"Yes, it is," the man said.

"Hello," Tom said. "This is Tom Ladd. Do you know my uncle, Ned Ladd?"

"Yes, I do," the man said. "Not very well, but I know him. I have met him."

"Well, Uncle Ned died last night of . . . of a heart attack."

"Really?" the man said. "That is too bad. Really too bad."

"Mr. Day, did you know anything about my uncle's work?" Tom asked.

"His work? Very little. Not much at all. He did not talk about it much," the man said.

"Oh. Well, we are still setting the day for the funeral. When I find out, I will . . ."

"Thank you. Good-bye," the man said. He hung up suddenly.

"Well, I am not getting very far," Tom thought. "And there is just one more number to try." He called the last number. "Hello. Is this Mr. Penn?" he asked.

"Yes, it is. What can I do for you?"

"This is Tom Ladd. I am calling about my Uncle Ned."

"Oh, yes," the man said. "Ned is a good friend."

"Well, I have to tell you that he is dead."

"Dead!"

"Yes. He died last night of a heart attack," Tom said.

"Oh, no," the man said. "That is too bad. We have lost a good man. A very, very good man. And his work . . ."

"Do you know about his work?" Tom asked. "You see, I never knew him very well. I would like to know about his work."

"Yes, I worked with him," the man said. "I do not know very much about it. But I would be glad to talk to you about what I do know. Come right over, my boy. Come right over."

Tom ran out of the house. He jumped in his car. Now he was getting somewhere! He drove away.

He did not see someone watching him from the window. He did not see someone turn and go up the stairs. He did not see someone go quietly into his room.

1. Comprehension Questions

Directions. Answer these questions about the story you have just read. Put an *x* in the box beside the best answer to each question.

1. Who was Trask?
(B) ☐ a. The cook
    ☐ b. The doctor
    ☐ c. The driver
    ☐ d. The policeman

2. How long had Tom been living with his uncle?
(B) ☐ a. For one day
    ☐ b. Not very long
    ☐ c. For five years
    ☐ d. All his life

3. What could Tom tell from looking at his uncle's den?
(D) ☐ a. His uncle did a lot of work.
    ☐ b. His uncle had put all his papers away.
    ☐ c. His uncle did most of his work somewhere else.
    ☐ d. His uncle did not have much work to do.

4. Who was the first one to find the body?
(C) ☐ a. The cook
    ☐ b. The police
    ☐ c. Tom
    ☐ d. Trask

5. Tom said, "There is <u>something funny</u> going on here.
(A) I think that my uncle has been murdered." What does
this mean?
    ☐ a. His uncle looks like he is happy.
    ☐ b. His uncle is not really dead.
    ☐ c. Something has happened to make them laugh.
    ☐ d. Something odd is going on.

6. Why did Tom think that his uncle had been murdered?
(D) ☐ a. He felt that Trask did not like his uncle.
    ☐ b. He knew that someone was after his uncle.
    ☐ c. He saw that there had been a fight.
    ☐ d. He thought that his uncle's face looked funny.

7. Tom said, "But he was my uncle. I am <u>all he had.</u>"
(A) What does this mean?
    ☐ a. His uncle did not have any money.
    ☐ b. His uncle's papers are not worth anything.
    ☐ c. Tom and his uncle had always been close.
    ☐ d. Tom is the only one left in the family.

8. Tom wanted to find out what his uncle was working on.
(E) Why?
    ☐ a. He wanted to do more of the same work himself.
    ☐ b. He wanted to find out if his uncle had been killed
       for it.
    ☐ c. He wanted to tell the police everything he could
       find out.
    ☐ d. He wanted to throw all of the old papers away.

9. Tom made some phone calls. His first call was to

(C) ☐ a. Mr. Day.

☐ b. Mr. Penn.

☐ c. a store.

☐ d. his uncle's lawyer.

10. What is this story most about?

(E) ☐ a. A missing tooth

☐ b. Finding Tom's uncle dead

☐ c. How Tom finds his uncle's friends

☐ d. How Tom looks for a job.

Skills Used to Answer Questions

A. Recognizing Words in Context   B. Recalling Facts

C. Keeping Events in Order   D. Making Inferences

E. Understanding Main Ideas

1. Language Skills

Vowel and Consonant Sounds

There are two kinds of letters. There are vowels and there are consonants.

Here are the vowels the way you see them printed:

       A E I O U   or   a e i o u

Here are the vowels written as capital letters: Copy them. Write your letter on the line under each letter.

a   *E*   *I*   *O*   *U*

_____ _____ _____ _____ _____

Here are the vowels written as small letters. Copy them. Write your letter on the line under each letter.

a   *e*   *i*   *o*   *u*

_____ _____ _____ _____ _____

Here are the vowels printed as block letters. Copy them. Print your letter on the line under each letter.

A   E   I   O   U

_____ _____ _____ _____ _____

The letter Y is sometimes a vowel. Copy it on the lines beside each way it is shown.

Y_____   y_____   *y*_____

All of the other letters are consonants. Here they are the way you see them printed:

B C D F G H J K L M N P Q R S T V W X Y Z
b c d f g h j k l m n p q r s t v w x y z

Copy the consonants on the lines as shown.

B _____	*b* _____	B _____
C _____	*c* _____	C _____
D _____	*d* _____	D _____
F _____	*f* _____	F _____
G _____	*g* _____	G _____
H _____	*h* _____	H _____
J _____	*j* _____	J _____
K _____	*k* _____	K _____
L _____	*l* _____	L _____
M _____	*m* _____	M _____
N _____	*n* _____	N _____
P _____	*p* _____	P _____
Q _____	*q* _____	Q _____
R _____	*r* _____	R _____
S _____	*s* _____	S _____

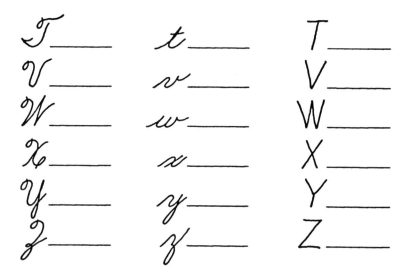

Most of the consonants have only one sound. But the vowels can have two sounds: a long sound and a short sound. If you want to sound out a word, you have to know if the vowel is long or short.

Here are the long vowel sounds. The long vowels have the same sounds as their names. Copy the words. Say the words as you write them and print them. Hear the sounds the long vowels make.

Long a as in day: *day* _____ DAY _____

Long e as in he: *he* _____ HE _____

Long i as in like: *like* _____ LIKE_____

Long o as in go: *go* _____ GO _____

Long u as in blue: *blue* _____ BLUE _____

Long y as in fly: *fly* _____ FLY _____

Here are the short vowel sounds. They are not like the long vowel sounds and have to be learned. Copy the words. Say the words as you write them and print them. Hear the sounds the short vowels make.

Short a as in man: *man* _____ MAN _____

Short e as in pet: *pet* _____ PET _____

Short i as in is: *is* _____ IS _____

Short o as in hot: *hot* _____ HOT _____

Short u as in up: *up* _____ UP _____

Short y as in gym: *gym* _____ GYM _____

Exercise 1

Look at the words below. On the first line next to each word, write the consonants that are in that word. On the next line, write the vowel. On the last line tell if the vowel is long (L) or short (S). Look at the examples in the box first.

Word	Consonants	Vowel	Sound
me	*m*	*e*	L
pin	*p, n*	*i*	S

1. on _____ _____ _____

2. ran _____ _____ _____

3. know _____ _____ _____

4. by _____ _____ _____

5. still _____ _____ _____

6. night _____ _____ _____

7. cup _____ _____ _____

8. no _____ _____ _____

9. next _____ _____ _____

10. Tom _____ _____ _____

Exercise 2

Look at the words below. On the first line next to each word, print the consonants. On the next line, print the vowel. On the last line, tell if the vowel is long (L) or short (S). Look at the examples in the box first.

Word	Consonants	Vowel	Sound
can	C,N	A	S
high	H,G,H	I	L

1. most   _____   _____   _____

2. tell   _____   _____   _____

3. kind   _____   _____   _____

4. last   _____   _____   _____

5. at   _____   _____   _____

6. fight   _____   _____   _____

7. best   _____   _____   _____

8. so   _____   _____   _____

9. sky   _____   _____   _____

10. shut   _____   _____   _____

1. Understanding Life Skills

Simple Directions

Every day we see directions and we have to follow them. When you drive, you have to read directions: NO LEFT TURN. When you walk, you have to read directions: CROSS ONLY AT CORNER. In fact, if you think about it, you have to read directions in almost everything you do: at work, when you shop, wherever you go.

If you know how to read directions and can follow them, you can save yourself extra time or extra work. A sign at the bank might say: FILL OUT SLIP BEFORE COMING TO WINDOW. If you do not read and follow this direction, you may have to wait in a long line and have to leave the line to go fill out the slip. Then you will have to go to the end of the line and wait again. In many ways, then, it can pay you to know how to read and follow directions.

Sometimes directions are short and simple, like the directions you saw above. Simple directions tell you to do, or not do, one thing. KEEP OFF THE GRASS is a simple direction.

Here is how to read and follow a simple direction:

1. Read it carefully.
2. Find the key word or key words.
3. Do it completely.

Read these simple directions. Find the key word in each one. It has a line under it.

DO NOT SMOKE. You will have to go somewhere else if you want to smoke.

PRINT YOUR NAME. Do not write or sign your name, print it.

SHAKE WELL <u>BEFORE</u> USING. Be sure you shake it first, before you use it.

Sometimes it is hard to tell which word is the key word. In the last direction above, SHAKE WELL BEFORE USING, every word is important. The key word could be SHAKE. Or it could be WELL. If you cannot find the key word right away, there may be more than one. Find all of the important words. Do what each word says.

Read these simple directions. Look for the key words. The key words will tell you what the direction really means. Answer the question with each direction. Print YES or NO on the line to show your answer.

1. PLEASE WALK IN. Should you wait for someone to open the door for you? _____

2. KEEP AWAY FROM HEAT. Should you keep this near a stove? _____

3. PLEASE WAIT FOR HOSTESS TO SEAT YOU. Should you stay where you are until someone comes to show you to a table? _____

4. LOOK BOTH WAYS BEFORE CROSSING. Do cars come from two directions on this street? _____

5. HAVE EXACT FARE READY. Will the driver change a five-dollar bill? _____

6. PRINT YOUR NAME AT THE TOP OF THE PAGE. Should anything go above your name? _____

7. FILL UP TO THIS LINE. Can you put too much in?

_____

8. DO NOT STORE IN DIRECT SUNLIGHT. Should you keep this away from a window? _____

9. KEEP OUT OF REACH OF CHILDREN. Should you give this to your baby? _____

10. WATCH YOUR STEP. Can you trip if you are not careful? _____

Try always to read directions carefully. Be sure you understand what you have to do.

1. Applying Life Skills

Following Simple Directions

Let us look at the way to read a short or simple direction:

1. Read it carefully.
2. Find the key word or key words.
3. Do it completely.

Use these steps to read and follow the directions below. Read each direction and then do what it says.

Exercise

1. Print in the box the name of the fifth month of the year.

```
┌─────────────────────────────────────────┐
│                                           │
│                                           │
└─────────────────────────────────────────┘
```

2. Put a line under the first word in this sentence.

3. Look at the title on the cover of this book. Write it on the line below.

_____

4. Below are six circles. Add enough circles to make ten.

◯ ◯ ◯ ◯ ◯ ◯

5. Copy the sentence below. Write it on the lines. Then draw a vertical line (/) between every word.

Always read and follow directions carefully.

_____

_____

6. Put quotation marks (" ") around the words that tell what Tom said.

> Tom said, I think my uncle was murdered.

7. In the circle below, write the number of this page.

8. On the line below, print in block letters the fiftn word in this sentence.

_____

9. Copy the sentence below. Write it. Put a comma (,) after the driver's name.

> Trask drive me home, please.

_____

10. Add enough lines to those below to make five squares.

11. Print the five vowels in the squares above. Put one vowel in each square.

12. Which sign below means NO SMOKING? Put an x in the right box.

13. Below are ten circles. Put an *x* in every other one. Start with the second circle.

14. Put an *x* through all of the odd numbers below.

1 2 3 4 5 6 7 8 9 10 11 12 13 14 15

15. There are five stories in this book. **Print** the title of Story 2 on the line below.

_____

2. Preview Words

Study the words in the box. Then read the sentences below with your teacher. Look carefully at the words with lines under them.

against	highway	none	screeched
bridge	jolt	pedal	skid
coming	kind	radio	spun
control	lab	river	using
death	lives	scare	walk

1. Ned wanted to make a new kind of motor, too.
2. I know that it used radio waves.
3. None of his other friends could tell me anything.
4. He lives near you, just two or three blocks away.
5. "Thank you for coming to see me," Mr. Penn said.
6. He pulled out on the highway.
7. At this speed, he would be at the river soon.
8. His MG could not make the turn to go over the bridge.
9. Someone was using his good old MG.
10. Tom was slammed against the side of the car.
11. He turned the wheel and tried to go with the skid.
12. The tires screeched.
13. The world spun around him.
14. Tom felt a jolt on the seat belt.
15. They would check into his uncle's death some more.
16. They said they would call the lab.
17. Did your gas pedal get stuck?
18. He did not want to scare her any more.
19. It was something that can control cars by radio waves.
20. "I think that I will walk," Tom said.

2. Someone Wants to Kill Me!

CHAPTER FOUR

Tom sat down to talk with his uncle's friend, Mr. Penn.

"Your uncle was very smart," Mr. Penn told Tom. "He was always working on new things. He could think of things that no one had ever thought of before."

"What kind of things did he work on?" Tom asked.

"Oh, new tools to help people in their work. But they were not the kind of tools that most people use. They were not saws or drills or tools like that. They were *more* than that."

"How?" Tom asked.

"How can I tell you? Let me see . . . Ned made one thing that you put in your car. It used light waves. It would keep the car from hitting things, like trees. He was still working on it. He wanted to make a car that would drive itself. Then you could just sit back and watch."

"Wow! A car that would drive itself!" Tom said.

"Yes," Mr. Penn said. "Ned wanted to make a new kind of motor, too. He wanted to make a car that would use less gas."

"Did he do it?" Tom asked. "That would be good! We need that now!"

"No, he never made one," Mr. Penn said. "He had some plans worked out. But then he started on something new. He must have been working on it when he died."

"What was that?" Tom asked.

"I never knew what it was," Mr. Penn said. "I was not working on it, and he did not talk about it much."

"Oh," Tom said. He felt sad. Would he *ever* find out?

"I do know something about it," Mr. Penn said. "I know that it used radio waves. Ned said that it was the biggest thing that he had ever worked on. He said that if he could get it to work, it would change the world."

"Wow!" Tom said.

"Yes, it would change the world. That is all I know. Oh . . . one more thing. The tool itself was very, very small."

"Very small! Where did he keep it?" Tom asked.

"I did not ask him," Mr. Penn said. "But he did say that he had the best place in the world. He said that no one would ever find it."

"Very small . . ." Tom said. "Was it so small that he could put it in a tooth?"

"In a tooth? What a thought! Yes, Ned could have made something that small. They make things very small these days. They make things small for space ships and things like that."

"Yes, they do," Tom said.

"But what a good place! In a tooth! Who would ever think to look there?"

"That is what I want to know," Tom said. "But I am so glad that you could tell me this much. None of his other friends could tell me anything about his work.

"Really? Who did you call?" Mr. Penn asked.

"Well, one of them has moved. The woman I talked to did not know where he was. And I talked to Mr. Day. He could not tell me anything."

"That is funny," Mr. Penn said. "I thought he had worked with Ned. Oh, well, maybe not. He lives near you, just two or three blocks away."

"Oh. I have never met him. Maybe he worked with Uncle Ned before I came," Tom said.

"Maybe. Well, is the funeral all set?" Mr. Penn asked.

"The lawyer is taking care of it. I will let you know," Tom said.

"I will be there. Thank you for coming to see me," Mr. Penn said.

"Thank you for all your help," Tom said.

When Tom got back to his uncle's house, the cook had his lunch all made. As she put it on the table, she asked, "Are you feeling OK now?"

"Yes," Tom said. "I went to see one of Uncle Ned's friends."

"Oh, how nice. Did you have a good talk?"

"Yes," Tom said. "He told me about some of the things my uncle was working on. He must have been a very smart man."

"Oh, yes, he was," the cook said. "I did not work for him for very long, but I could tell that he was smart. He made all kinds of things. It is so sad. The world has lost a good man."

"Yes, it is sad," Tom said.

"Mr. Ladd, do you . . . do you . . ." the cook started to ask.

"What?"

"Do you still think that your uncle was murdered?"

"I do not know," Tom said. "I just do not know."

After lunch, Tom was very tired. He had been up most of the night. He went up to his room. He sat down on his bed.

Then he saw the note.

It said:

Watch out. Your uncle is dead.
You could be, too.

Tom jumped up. He looked around the room. Then he ran down the hall and down the stairs.

"Mr. Ladd! What is it?" asked the cook when she saw his face.

"Where is Trask?" Tom asked.

"He has gone out. Do you need him? I can call him," the cook said.

"No, no. I do not need him," Tom said. "And I do not think I will. I have my car. And I think it would be best for me to drive it myself."

CHAPTER FIVE

Tom called the police. He told them about the note. A policeman came to the house and looked around. Then he left, taking the note with him.

Tom went back upstairs. He tried again to get some sleep. But he could not get to sleep.

He kept thinking that he could hear something. He would sit up fast in his bed. He would look all around. But there would be nothing there. Then he would try again to get to sleep. But then he would think that he could hear something again.

At last he gave up. He got up and went downstairs. He went back into his uncle's den. He looked at his uncle's books again.

Now that he had talked to Mr. Penn, Tom knew what to look for. Yes, here was a book on radio waves. This book was on radio waves, too. And here was a book on cars. This one was on car motors. "Now I am getting somewhere," Tom thought.

Tom looked at the books for a long time. He tried to read them. He tried to read the notes that his uncle had put in the books. He started to find out a little more. But it was not much.

Some of the notes had Penn's name on them. Tom was glad to think of him working with his uncle.

Then Tom found one more book. It had not been used for a long time. In it were some notes with Day's name on them.

"That is funny," Tom said to himself. "I thought Mr. Day said that he did not work with Uncle Ned."

Just then the cook stuck her head in the door. "Would you like something?" she asked. "Your uncle liked a cup of tea when he was working."

"No, thank you," Tom said. "I have been at it for a long time. I think I will go for a drive."

"Do you want Trask to drive you in the Rolls?" the cook asked.

"No, no. I will take my car," Tom said quickly.

"Have a nice time," the cook said.

As Tom went outside, he looked all around. No Trask. He looked at his MG. He looked under the hood. Everything seemed to be all right.

Tom pulled out into the street. The car was running well. It was good to get out.

He drove for two or three blocks. Then he drove around the block. He checked in back of him. No one was in back of him.

He felt better. He did not want to think about anything. He just wanted to have a good time. He put the top of the car down. He turned on his radio. He sat back in his seat and just drove along, watching the streets go by.

He pulled out on the highway. He drove faster. The road rolled under him, faster and faster. The wind pushed at his hair. It felt good to have a good car.

Then he could hear something. It was a very small sound. A little click.

And he was not driving the car any more.

The car was driving itself.

Tom grabbed at the wheel. He turned it hard. But the car drove on.

He stepped on the brake. The car drove on.

What was going on? How could his good old MG take over like this?

He pulled the wheel this way and that. But the car just drove on.

Then he saw that the car was going faster. And faster. He was going 80 mph . . . 90 . . . 100 . . .

Suddenly Tom thought of something. The river! At this speed, he would be at the river very soon.

At this speed, even his MG could not make the turn to go over the bridge.

Someone wanted to kill him. And someone was using his good old MG to do it.

The car went faster and faster. The wind rushed past Tom's head. What could he do? He could not jump out at that speed. What could he do? He tried to think . . .

100 mph . . . 110 mph . . .

Suddenly he thought of something. He grabbed for the radio and turned it off.

Screech! Tom was slammed against the side of the car as it spun out. The wheel! He grabbed the wheel . . . It was his again. He turned the wheel and tried to go with the skid. The tires screeched . . . the world spun around him . . . he was going over . . .

The car rolled over. Tom felt a jolt on the seat belt. His

head slammed against the seat. The world spun around and around.

At last it stopped. The car was right side up, a little way from the highway. Cars were stopping and people were jumping out. Hands grabbed at him, getting him out of his seat belt.

"Are you all right?" someone asked. "Are you all right?"

"Yes. Yes, I think so," Tom said.

"You are lucky you have a roll bar!" someone said. "That roll bar saved you."

A police car pulled up. "OK," the policeman said, "what happened?"

"I wish I knew," Tom said.

CHAPTER SIX

"How fast were you going?" the policeman asked.

"100 mph, I think," Tom said.

"100 mph? Are you *crazy?*" the policeman asked. "Have you been drinking? We will have to check you out."

"No, wait," Tom said. "I have not been drinking. Someone is trying to kill me!"

"Someone is trying to kill you?" the policeman asked. "You are doing fine by yourself."

"No, let me tell you. Someone took over my car with radio waves."

"With radio waves?" The policeman gave Tom a funny look. Suddenly he said, "Hey, you are the one who said his uncle was murdered!"

"Yes, he was!" Tom said. "And now they are trying to kill me!"

"You will have to come down to the station with me," the policeman said.

"Do you have a radio in your car?" Tom asked.

"Yes. I will call a truck to get your car."

"OK. Call the truck. Then turn the radio off," Tom said.

"Turn the radio off? I never do that," the policeman said.

"You have to!" Tom said. "The radio waves! That is how they took over my car!"

"Well, we will have to risk it," the policeman said, looking at Tom. "I never turn off that radio."

All the way to the station, Tom was waiting for the little click. But it did not come.

At the police station, Tom told all about what had happened to him. Some of the police thought he was crazy. But some of them thought he might be right.

They told Tom that they would check into his uncle's death some more. They said they would call the lab and ask them to check again to find out why his uncle had died. Then one of them drove Tom home.

When Tom went into the house, the cook was waiting for him. "Do you want your supper now?" she asked.

"No, thank you," Tom said. "I do not feel like eating."

"Did you have a nice drive?"

"Well, no. I cracked up my car. They had to get a truck to take it away."

"Oh, no! Are you all right?" the cook asked. "What happened?"

"Well . . ." What could he say? What could he tell her? The police thought he was crazy. Now this nice old woman would think he was crazy, too.

"I was going too fast," he said at last.

"You were going too fast? That does not seem like something you would do." The cook looked very sad. Tom knew that she liked him. He knew that she did not want to think of him as a bad driver.

Tom did not want to see her look so sad. "I did not mean to go so fast," he said. "Something happened to my car."

"Something happened to your car?" The cook looked scared. "What happened? I mean . . . I do not know much about cars, but . . . Did your gas pedal get stuck or something?"

"No, it was not the gas pedal," Tom said. He looked down at the cook. What could he tell her? He did not want to scare her any more.

But maybe he *should* tell her. Maybe he should tell her what was going on. Then if something happened . . . If someone came for him in the night . . . It would be good to know that someone was watching out for him.

"I think that someone is trying to kill me," Tom said.

"Trying to kill you? Oh, no!" The cook started to cry.

"Now, now. You must not cry. They will not get me," Tom said.

"But why would someone want to kill you?" the cook asked.

"Someone killed my uncle. I just know it. He was working on something big, and they killed him for it. I am trying to find out what it was. And now they are trying to stop me." Tom told her about the note he had found in his bed. Then he told her about what happened in the car.

"It just went click?" the cook asked. "Just like that? And then the car ran away with you?"

"Yes. I think I know now what my uncle was working on."

"What?"

"Something that can control cars by radio waves," Tom said.

"By radio waves!"

"Yes. If the car radio is on, this thing can drive the car. From a long way away, I think."

"But why would your uncle want to crack up someone's car?" the cook asked.

"I do not think he wanted to crack up someone's car. He wanted to make cars safer. And this would not even need a driver. But someone killed him and took the control."

"But I have not seen anything like that control around here," the cook said.

"No, you would not have seen it. It was very small. It was so small that he kept it in his tooth," Tom said.

"In his tooth! Then . . ."

"Yes," Tom said, "that is why he was missing a tooth. That is why he looked so funny. Someone killed him. Then when he was dead, they took his tooth. They took his tooth and left him with his mouth open."

"Oh, the poor man," the cook said sadly.

"Yes. What a way to go!"

"Oh! Then I came in!" the cook said. "I must have scared them away!" She looked very scared again.

"Yes. You must be right," Tom said.

"And then I screamed. And then Trask . . ."

"Yes. What about Trask?" Tom asked.

"He came right away when I screamed," the cook said.

"Right away? How well do you know Trask? What kind of a man is he?" Tom asked.

"I do not know him very well," the cook said. "I have not worked here for very long. But he has worked here for a long time. He knew everything there was to know about your uncle. He knew your uncle better than his friends did."

Tom did not want to ask anything more. He did not want to scare the cook any more. "By the way, where is Trask?" was all he said.

"He is in his room," the cook said.

"What did he do today?" Tom asked.

"He went out in your uncle's Rolls. He said there was something he had to do. Do you want him? Now that you . . . you do not have your car any more, he can drive you."

"I think that I will walk," Tom said. "It will be good for me."

The cook started to go out of the room. Then she turned around again and looked at him. "You do not know who killed your uncle?" she asked.

What should he say? He did not *know* . . . he just *thought* he knew. "No. I do not know," he said at last.

"Maybe you should stop now," the cook said. "Maybe you should not look any more. If someone *is* trying to get you . . . They did not get you this time. But maybe next time . . . You should stop now. Will you?"

"No. I have to go on looking. I have to find out who killed my uncle," Tom said.

The cook went out, looking very sad. Tom felt bad that he had scared her and made her sad. She was a nice old woman. It was too bad to scare her. But it was good to know that someone cared about him.

2. Comprehension Questions

Directions. Answer these questions about the story you have just read. Put an *x* in the box beside the best answer to each question.

1. Ned Ladd wanted to make
(B) □ a. a car that would drive itself.
□ b. a car that would go fast.
□ c. a drill that worked by light waves.
□ d. a new kind of space ship.

2. Ned Ladd, Tom's uncle, was working on something that
(A) could change the world. What does this mean?
□ a. Ned Ladd's plans were out of this world.
□ b. The thing is very great.
□ c. The thing would not be worth very much.
□ d. The world is bad and needs changing.

3. When he died, Ned Ladd was working on something that
(C) □ a. used less gas.
□ b. used light waves.
□ c. used radio waves.
□ d. used a special motor.

4. The note said: "Watch out. Your uncle is dead. You
(A) could be, too." What does the note really mean?
□ a. Do not drive your car any more.
□ b. Do not talk to your uncle's friends.
□ c. Stop looking into your uncle's death.
□ d. Trask killed your uncle.

5. Why could Tom not get to sleep?

(D) ☐ a. He could hear too many sounds from the street.

☐ b. He did not want Trask to come into his room.

☐ c. He wanted to look at his uncle's books.

☐ d. The note had made him scared.

6. What did Tom find in an old book?

(B) ☐ a. The notes with Day's name on them.

☐ b. The place where the control was kept.

☐ c. The plans for a new kind of gas.

☐ d. The way light waves work.

7. What did Tom hear just before he lost control of his car?

(C) ☐ a. A little click

☐ b. A police car radio

☐ c. Music on his car radio

☐ d. The wind rushing by

8. How did someone try to kill Tom?

(E) ☐ a. By fixing the brakes on his MG

☐ b. By making him crash into other cars

☐ c. By pushing his car into the water

☐ d. By taking over his car with radio waves

9. Why did Tom tell the cook that someone was trying to

(D) kill him?

☐ a. He did not like her, and he wanted to scare her.

☐ b. He knew that she was smart, and she could take care of herself.

☐ c. He liked her, and he wanted her to look after him.

☐ d. He thought that she could tell him who was trying to kill him.

10. Tom thought he knew why his uncle's tooth was missing.
(E) What did he think?

   ☐ a. He did not know his uncle well and did not see it before.

   ☐ b. He lost a tooth in the fight when someone killed him.

   ☐ c. His uncle took his tooth out so Tom would know he had been killed.

   ☐ d. Someone knew the tooth had the control in it and took it.

Skills Used to Answer Questions

A. Recognizing Words in Context   B. Recalling Facts

C. Keeping Events in Order   D. Making Inferences

E. Understanding Main Ideas

2. Language Skills

Vowel and Consonant Patterns

Most of the time you can tell if a vowel is long or short. You can tell by looking at the *patterns* for long and short vowels.

The best way to look at these patterns is to use letters to stand for the vowels and consonants. **V** stands for any vowel. **C** stands for any consonant, or more than one consonant.

Pattern 1: C − V (Consonant–Vowel). Words with this pattern have a vowel at the end with one or two consonants in front of it. When a word has this pattern, the vowel is long.

Copy these pattern 1 words. Write them and print them. The first one has been done for you.

go	he	she	so	by

C − V

go _____   _____   _____   _____

C − V

GO _____   _____   _____   _____

Next, put the letters **C** and **V** above the consonants and vowels to show that these words fit pattern 1. See how the first one has been done.

Now, say each word to yourself. Hear the long vowels.

58

Pattern 2: C−V−V−C (Consonant−Vowel−Vowel−Consonant). This pattern has two vowels side by side, with one or two consonants on both ends. When a word has this pattern, the first vowel is long. You do not hear the other vowel at all.

Copy these pattern 2 words. Write them and print them. The first one has been done for you.

C−V−V−C   C−V−V−C

soap   *soap*   SOAP

seem   _____   _____

leap   _____   _____

chain   _____   _____

died   _____   _____

Next, put the letters **C** and **V** over the consonants and vowels to show that these words fit pattern 2. See how the first one has been done.

Now, say each word to yourself. Hear the long vowels.

Pattern 3: C—V—C—V (Consonant—Vowel—Consonant—Vowel). This pattern has a consonant and a vowel and then another consonant and a vowel. When a word has this pattern, the first vowel is long. The last vowel is an *e* and you do not hear it.

Copy these pattern 3 words. Write them and print them. The first one has been done for you.

C-V-C-V   C-V-C-V

fuse   *fuse*   FUSE

these   _____   _____

late   _____   _____

broke   _____   _____

time   _____   _____

Next, put the letters **C** and **V** over the consonants and vowels to show that these words fit pattern 3. See how the first one has been done.

Next, say the words to yourself. Hear the long vowels.

Pattern 4: C−V−C or V−C (Consonant−Vowel−Consonant or Vowel−Consonant). This pattern tells you that the vowel is short. If there is only one vowel, and there are one or more consonants after the vowel, the vowel will be short.

Copy these pattern 4 words. Write them and print them. The first one has been done for you.

	C-V-C-C	C-V-C-C
dent	*dent*	DENT
on		
ask		
spill		
cut		

Next, put **C** and **V** over the consonants and vowels to show that these words fit pattern 4. See how the first one has been done.

Now, say the words to yourself. Hear the short vowels.

Exercise

Copy these words. Print them. Tell what the pattern is. Then tell if the vowel sound (the vowel you can hear) is long (L) or short (S). The first two have been done.

Word	Print	Pattern	Vowel Sound
1. got	*GOT*	4	S
2. cake	*CAKE*	3	L
3. but			
4. cup			
5. thank			
6. next			
7. note			
8. suit			
9. nice			
10. stop			
11. boat			
12. if			

13. left _____ _____ _____

14. no _____ _____ _____

15. fell _____ _____ _____

16. stone _____ _____ _____

17. made _____ _____ _____

18. top _____ _____ _____

19. big _____ _____ _____

20. mean _____ _____ _____

2. Understanding Life Skills

Long Directions

At the end of Story 1, we saw how to read and follow simple, or short, directions.

Directions are not always short and simple. Sometimes they are long and not so easy to read. Instead of just a few words, there are times when directions are three and four lines long.

You have to know how to read long directions if you want to get along. Many things come with long directions and you have to know how to handle them.

Here is an example of some long directions. These directions tell you how to buy something you have seen in a catalog.

Call in your order toll free. Dial 1-800-555-1212. Items can be charged to Master Charge, VISA, American Express or sent COD. Orders shipped 4th class mail or UPS. $1.75 shipping and handling charge will be added to your order.

Here is the best way to handle long directions:

1. Read the directions all the way through.
2. Change them into a number of short or simple directions.
3. Follow each one as if it were a simple direction.
        a. Read it carefully.
        b. Find the key word or key words.
        c. Do it completely.

Let us see how this works with the long directions we have just read.

First, read the directions again, all the way through.

Next, change them into a number of short directions. The numbers below show all of the short directions we can make. Read each one carefully. Find any key words. Answer the question that follows each short direction. Print your answers.

1. Call in your order toll free. This first direction tells you two things. (1) You can use the telephone to place your order. You do not have to mail in. (2) The call will not cost you anything. The company you are buying from will pay for the call. Which two words tell you that you do not have to pay for the call?

_____   _____

2. Dial 1-800-555-1212. This is the number to call to order the thing you want. Which word tells you that you can make the call yourself without using the operator?

3. Items can be charged to Master Charge, VISA, American Express or sent COD. You can use any one of these 3 credit cards to pay for your order. Have the card ready when you call so that you can give the number that is on it. If you do not have these credit cards, you can pay the mailman when he brings your order. Which three letters mean that you can pay CASH ON DELIVERY?

4. Orders shipped 4th class mail or UPS. UPS is a company that brings small packages to your home by truck. Someone will have to be at home when the UPS driver comes. He will ask you to sign your name when he gives you the package. UPS does not go everywhere. Your package may come by mail. What class of mail is used for packages?

_____   _____   _____

5. $1.75 shipping and handling charge will be added to your order. The company will charge you for the cost of putting what you have ordered in a box and sending it to you. How much more will you have to pay for this?

$ _____

If you use these steps when you have to read long directions, you will find that they are easy to read and follow every time.

2. Applying Life Skills

Following Long Directions

Look back at the pages that tell the best way to read long directions. Read these pages again if you need to before going on to this exercise.

Shown below are the directions for using a new kind of bathroom scale. This is a *digital* scale, one that shows numbers without a dial.

Read the directions and answer the questions. Use what you know about making short directions out of long ones to help you.

Using Your Scale

This digital scale works best on a hard, flat surface. The scale turns on by itself when 25 pounds of weight are put on it. The scale will read weights from 25 pounds up to 300 pounds. Do not put more than 300 pounds on the scale. This is too much weight; it will damage the scale.

To weigh yourself, step on the scale. Keep your weight spread as evenly as possible and stand very still. The window in the scale will show only zeroes for about 5 seconds. Then the numbers will flash. They will change and then stop when they reach your weight.

Questions

1. Where will this scale work best? Put an *x* in the right box.

☐ a. On a wood floor
☐ b. On a rubber mat
☐ c. On a thick rug

2. Is there a switch to turn on the scale? Circle your answer.

Yes   No   Directions do not say

3. What is the smallest weight that will show on the scale? Circle your answer.

10 pounds   25 pounds   50 pounds

4. Will any harm be done if too much weight is put on the the scale? Circle your answer.

Yes   No   Directions do not say

5. Which one of these persons should *not* get on the scale? Put an *x* in the right box.
□ a. Someone who weighs 210 pounds
□ b. Someone who weighs 290 pounds
□ c. Someone who weighs 310 pounds

6. Do the directions tell you how much harm will be done to the scale if you put too much weight on it? Circle your answer.

Yes   No

7. Is it all right to stand on one corner of the scale? Circle your answer.

Yes   No   Directions do not say

8. How long does it take for the scale to show your weight? Put an *x* in the right box.

☐ a. One second

☐ b. 5 to 10 seconds

☐ c. About a minute

9. How does this scale show your weight? Put an *x* in the right box.

☐ a. Numbers show in a window.

☐ b. A pointer moves on a dial.

☐ c. A voice calls out your weight.

10. What kind of use do you think this scale will give? Put an *x* in the right box.

☐ a. Light use for one year

☐ b. Normal use

☐ c. Extra heavy-duty use

3. Preview Words

Study the words in the box. Then read the sentences below with your teacher. Look carefully at the words with lines under them.

another	downtown	hurt	slept
auto	everywhere	known	sometimes
city	ground	louder	sounded
closer	helpless	quit	tomorrow
crashed	higher	rolling	without

1. Maybe he should get out of the city.
2. He looked down at the ground.
3. It was getting closer.
4. The radio got louder as the truck got closer.
5. The DJ sounded so happy.
6. It crashed into the house.
7. The door crashed in, wood falling, glass flying everywhere.
8. Sometimes people think of things later.
9. He might have known where I was today.
10. We can not keep him there without more to go on.
11. He stopped downtown and got something to eat.
12. He slept well for the first time in days.
13. Do you want me to quit?
14. The funeral will be tomorrow at 2:00.
15. He felt so helpless.
16. He went to the auto body shop.
17. The tow truck came in with another car.
18. Higher and higher he went, fighting to get free.
19. The truck was rolling faster.
20. He hurt all over.

3. The Radio

CHAPTER SEVEN

Tom had a bad night again. He was thinking about his uncle and about his car. "I will have to get some sleep," he thought, "or I will crack up."

Just as it got light, he got up. He went quietly down the stairs and out the door.

Quietly, he went out to his uncle's big Rolls. He looked back at the house. Good. If Trask woke up, he could not see the car from the house.

Very slowly, Tom opened the door of the car. He looked in. The Rolls was so big, and there were so many places to hide things. How would he ever find something as small as a tooth?

He had to try. Trask must have it somewhere.

Tom looked on the seats. He looked under the seats. He looked on the floor. He looked under the floor mats. He felt down in back of the dash.

Maybe he could see something under the car. He got out and started to get under the car. But wait! It was getting late. The cook must be up by now. She would be getting breakfast. Then Trask would come out.

Tom could not risk it. He walked slowly away from the car.

He started to go into the house. But he did not feel like eating. He turned around and walked down the street.

The street was very quiet.

He walked sadly along. He felt bad. What could he do? Where could he go? Now he did not even want to go home.

Maybe the cook was right. Maybe he should get out of the city. He wanted to find out who had killed his uncle. But did

STORY 3

he want to risk getting killed himself? Maybe he should run for it now, while he still could.

It was getting later. Cars started to go by, more and more of them. "Look at all those lucky people," Tom thought. *"They* are not scared to go home."

He walked slowly along. He looked down at the ground so that he would not have to look at the people in the cars. He tried to think about what to do.

A small truck passed him and pulled over to the side of the street. The driver jumped out and opened the back of the truck. He took out some boxes. Tom walked past him, not looking at him. "Lucky!" he thought as he walked on. "He has nothing to be scared of. He has nothing to do but drive those boxes around all day. He just plays his radio and . . ."

His radio!

Tom turned around fast. The truck was coming at him. Tom was too scared to move.

"Hey!" the driver shouted. "My truck! Watch out!"

That did it. Tom ran. And the truck was right in back of him.

The truck rolled down the street after Tom. Tom turned and ran to someone's house. The truck ran right up on the grass after him.

Tom could see that he would not have time to get into the house. He ran around the house, with the truck right in back of him. It was getting closer.

Tom ran in back of a tree. The truck rushed past him. It turned, making big marks in the grass, and came for him again.

A man opened the door of the house. "What is going on?" he shouted. Tom ran for the house. The truck was right in back of him. It was coming faster and faster. Tom could hear the radio playing. The radio got louder as the truck got closer. The DJ sounded so happy.

Tom ran up the stairs to the house. The man shouted and tried to grab him. But Tom grabbed the man and pulled him inside.

The truck was coming too fast to stop. It crashed into the house.

Tom pulled the man away from the door. The door crashed in, wood falling, glass flying everywhere. But the truck was stopped.

"What are you *doing?*" shouted the man. "Are you *crazy?* My door! My house! I will get you for this!"

"Hey, I did not do it!" Tom shouted. "That truck was after me! It was trying to kill me! Get the man in the truck!"

"I am going to call the police!" the man shouted.

"Yes, do that!" Tom said. He sat down. He felt so tired.

The man with the boxes ran up. "Hey, what did you do to my truck?" he shouted.

"What did *I* do?" Tom asked. "Your truck went crazy! I could have been killed!"

"I had the brake on," the man said. "What happened? That truck did not just roll. It went all around the house!"

"I told you," Tom said. "It went crazy."

They just looked at the truck. It was stuck in a pile of wood and glass where the door had been. They could hear the DJ saying, "And now the news . . ."

"Turn that radio off," Tom said quietly.

CHAPTER EIGHT

When the police came, they took one look at Tom. "You again!" they said.

"Yes, me again," Tom said. "I tell you, someone is trying to kill me!"

Tom told them the story about the truck. Then they talked to the man in the house and the man with the boxes.

"Well, you must be right," they said at last. "It is not every day that a truck goes out of its way to run someone down. Now, do you know who it is?"

"No," Tom said.

"Did you see anyone near you? Today, and when you were in your car, was there anyone around?"

"No, I did not see anyone. I was not looking. I was just trying not to get killed," Tom said. "But there is someone who might be in on it."

"Who?" the police asked.

"My uncle's driver, Trask."

"Why do you think he is in on it?" they asked.

"Well," Tom said, "the killers would need to have someone in the house. They would need someone who knew my uncle well. He could tell them what my uncle was doing every day. And my uncle would know him and not be scared of him."

"Yes, you might be right," a policeman said. "They might have had someone in the house. But why Trask?"

"On the night of the murder," Tom said, "Trask was there fast . . . too fast. It was at night, but he was there right away. Then, you asked Trask about my uncle's tooth. First he said that he had never looked. Then, later, he said that he knew it was gone."

"Well," said the policeman, "sometimes people think of things later."

"I know," Tom said. "But now . . . well, he keeps watching me. And he could have left that note on my bed."

"Yes, he could have."

"And the cook said he was out of the house when my car took me for a ride. And he might have known where I was today."

"OK, OK," the policeman said. "We will pick him up and take him down to the station. We will ask him about these things. But we can not keep him there without more to go on."

"I know," Tom said. "But it will give me a little time to rest."

"Yes. Now, what about the cook?" the policeman asked.

"What about her?"

"Well, she is someone in the house," the policeman said. "She knew your uncle and he knew her. Do you think she was in on it?"

"The cook? No, no!" Tom said. "She could not have been in on it. She is just a nice old woman. She is scared of everything. No, she could not have been in on it. Not her."

"All right," the policeman said. "But it could not have been Trask alone. He would not have known what your uncle was working on. It had to be someone who knew his work. What do you think?"

"How would I know?" Tom asked. "I did not live with him very long. I do not know anything about his work. I just want Trask out of there so I can get some rest!"

"OK, OK," the policeman said. "Go on home. Get some rest. But if anything happens . . . look around!"

"Yes. Yes, I will," Tom said.

Tom was so tired. "What a day," he thought. "No sleep, no breakfast, that truck. And the day is not over yet."

He stopped downtown and got something to eat. Then he went home.

The cook was waiting for him at the door. She was crying again. "The police came and took Trask away," she said. "He did not do anything, did he?"

"The police just wanted to ask him some things. He will be home again soon," Tom told her. "He will be home too soon," he thought to himself.

"Oh, dear," said the cook. "First your uncle, and then your car, and now this. Oh dear, oh dear. It all scares me so much."

"There, there," Tom said. "It will be all right." He did not tell her about the truck.

"And here you are, you poor boy. You did not get any breakfast. Can I get you something to eat?"

"No, I ate downtown. I just want to go to bed," Tom said.

"Yes, you poor thing, you must be tired," the cook said.

"Will you wake me up when Trask gets home?" Tom asked.

"Yes, I will."

Tom went upstairs and went to bed. He slept well for the first time in days.

Suddenly he woke up. Someone was in the room. It was Trask!

Tom sat up fast. What could he do? Was this the end?

"What do you want?" he asked.

"The cook said that you wanted to see me when I got home," Trask said.

"Oh! Yes, I did. I . . . um . . . What did the police want?" Tom asked.

"They just asked me about the night your uncle died. They asked me about what I was doing now."

"Oh," Tom said.

"Mr. Ladd?" Trask said.

"Yes?"

"Do you want me to quit? I mean, there is not much for me to do, now that your uncle is not here."

"No, no, that is all right," Tom said quickly. "Not right away. Wait till . . . till things get worked out."

"All right. Will that be all, Mr. Ladd?"

"Yes. Thank you," Tom said.

When Trask left, Tom lay down on the bed again. He felt as if he had been running fast.

"If Trask quit, then I would never know where he was," Tom said to himself. "But how can I live in the same house with that man?"

CHAPTER NINE

The phone rang. The cook called up to Tom. "It is for you, Mr. Ladd."

Who could it be? Would it be the police lab with news about his uncle's death? Tom got up and went into the next room. He picked up the phone. It was his uncle's lawyer.

"Hello, Mr. Ladd," the lawyer said. "Everything is all set for the funeral. It will be tomorrow at 2:00."

"Good," said Tom. "Thank you for taking care of all that."

"That is all right," the lawyer said. "Did you get the names of your uncle's friends? Would you like me to call them to tell them about the funeral?"

"That would be very nice. I have talked to some of them. But I just do not feel like making any more calls." He gave the lawyer the names and phone numbers that he had.

"Oh, yes, Mr. Day," the lawyer said. "He and your uncle were very close friends. Mr. Day worked with your uncle a lot."

"He did? But he said . . ."

"Then they had a fight," the lawyer went on. "Your uncle would not let Mr. Day work with him any more. He got rid of all Mr. Day's papers. It was very sad."

"Yes, it must have been sad," Tom said.

"So I do not know if he will come to the funeral," the lawyer said. "But I will call him."

"Thank you," Tom said. "Good-bye." He hung up the phone. So that was why Mr. Day had sounded so funny when he called him. "He must feel very bad, now that Uncle Ned is dead," Tom thought. It was too bad.

Tom felt very sad. He just wanted to get out of the house. He grabbed something to eat by himself. Then he went out.

He walked downtown, looking at all the cars that went by. He felt sad about his uncle. And every time he could hear a car radio playing, he felt sick.

What could he do? He felt so helpless. "I thought I could find out what my uncle was working on," he said to himself. "I thought I could find out who killed him. Right. Now I am scared to stay home. Now I do not know what to do with myself. Man, oh man. What a life."

Tom walked along, trying to think of what to do. At last he thought, "I know. I will go see about my car."

He went to the auto body shop. There was his poor little MG with the doors off. "You look like I feel," he told the car.

He walked around the body shop. He looked at all the cars. He thought about what had happened to them. "I was lucky," he thought. "My car is not as bad as some of them."

The tow truck came in with another car. The men took the car off the hook and pushed it away. Tom watched them. It was all there was to do.

Suddenly there was a little click.

At the same time, something grabbed him! He was pulled up off his feet. He was hanging in the air. Higher and higher he went, fighting to get free.

"Hey!" shouted one of the men. "Get off that hook!"

"Help me! Help me!" Tom shouted.

The hook started to swing. Tom was swinging with it.

The men came running up. They grabbed at Tom. "Help me!" Tom shouted.

The truck started to roll.

It was backing up. It was going for the wall of the body shop.

"Hey!" one of the men shouted. "Stop that truck!"

"Turn off the radio!" Tom shouted. "Turn off the radio!"

One of the men jumped into the truck. He stepped on the brake. "It will not stop!" he shouted.

The truck was rolling faster. Tom was swinging on the hook. The wall was coming at him.

"Turn off the radio!" Tom shouted again. "Tell him to turn off the radio!"

The wall was so close he could almost feel it.

The man in the truck turned off the radio.

The truck stopped. The hook swung out. Tom hit the wall and then fell off the hook. He lay on the ground. He hurt all over. He could not get up yet.

The men came running up. "Are you OK?" they asked. They helped him stand up. "Are you OK now?"

"Call the police!" Tom said.

"Hey, man," one of the men said, "that truck was parked! I do not know how you got on that hook. But you are all right. You do not need to call the police."

"No, wait," Tom said. "I am not mad at you. But someone is trying to kill me. Someone is using a radio to control cars and trucks. They can make the cars and trucks try to kill me."

The men looked scared. "You mean . . ." one of them said. "Is that why the truck stopped when I turned off the radio?"

"You got it," Tom said.

"And that is your MG! You are the one who rolled the MG!"

"Well," said Tom, "my MG rolled me. I was lucky. If I had not turned off the radio, I would have been killed."

"OK. We will call the police," the men said.

The police came quickly. They asked the men what had happened.

One policeman asked, "Did you see anyone? Was anyone hanging around? Did you see any cars go by?"

"No," said one of the men. "We were all trying to stop the truck."

"Think!" the policeman said. "Try to think! Anything will help!"

"Well," said one of the men, "two or three cars went by. But I did not look at them."

"Did any of them stop?" the policeman asked.

"No, I do not think so. It has been slow around here. Just that blue van parked across the street. But that was here when we pulled in with the truck."

"What blue van?" Tom asked.

"That one . . . hey, it is gone!"-

"Did you see anyone get into it?" the policeman asked.

"No. There was no one around," the man said.

"OK. Tell me about the van," the policeman said.

"Well, it was . . . you know . . . it was a van. A blue one. A Ford, I think. It looked new. No windows in the back. Red seats, I think. That is all I can think of."

"Did any of you see it?" the policeman asked the other men.

"Yes," said one. "It had a CB radio."

"OK. We will look for it," the policeman said. "Tom, you should come with me."

"Good-bye," the men from the body shop told Tom. "Good luck!"

"Hey, man," one of the men called after him, "do you want me to take the radio out of your car?"

3. Comprehension Questions

Directions. Answer these questions about the story you have just read. Put an *x* in the box beside the best answer to each question.

1. When the truck ran into the house, what did the man in
(D) the house think?
  □ a. The man with the boxes was after them.
  □ b. Tom had wanted the truck to hit the house.
  □ c. Tom was just running around to be funny.
  □ d. Tom was lucky not to have been killed.

2. "It is not every day that a truck goes out of its way to
(A) run someone down." What does this mean?
  □ a. A truck does not often go out of its way.
  □ b. The brake must not have been on all the way.
  □ c. The driver should keep his truck off the grass.
  □ d. The truck must have been under the control of someone.

3. When did the police start to believe Tom?
(C) □ a. After the tow truck picked him up.
  □ b. After the truck crashed into the house.
  □ c. When they saw the blue van nearby.
  □ d. When Tom could not find anything in the Rolls.

4. What do the police now believe?
(E) □ a. Someone really can control a car by radio waves.
  □ b. The men in the auto body shop went after Tom with a tow truck.
  □ c. Tom just thinks someone is trying to kill him.
  □ d. Trask is the one who murdered Tom's uncle.

5. "When Trask left, Tom lay down on the bed again. He
(A) felt as if he had been running fast." How did Tom feel?

    ☐ a. Happy   ☐ c. Scared

    ☐ b. Sad   ☐ d. Scared

6. What did Tom think about the cook?

(B) ☐ a. She had been in on the murder, too.

    ☐ b. She had not been in the house when Tom's uncle
        was killed.

    ☐ c. She knew who had murdered Tom's uncle.

    ☐ d. She was too old and scared to have been in on the
        murder.

7. Why did the lawyer think that Day would not come to
(D) the funeral?

    ☐ a. Mr. Day did not like Tom.

    ☐ b. Mr. Day had not been a close friend of Tom's uncle.

    ☐ c. Mr. Day had too much of his own work to do.

    ☐ d. Mr. Day would still be mad at Tom's uncle.

8. What happened when Tom went to the auto body shop?

(C) ☐ a. He was grabbed by a policeman in the street.

    ☐ b. He was grabbed by the driver of the blue van.

    ☐ c. He was grabbed by the hook on the tow truck.

    ☐ d. He was grabbed by two men at the body shop.

9. Who told the police about the blue van?

(B) ☐ a. The man with the boxes.

    ☐ b. The man in the house.

    ☐ c. The men in the body shop.

    ☐ d. Tom, after he got off the hook.

10. What main thing did Tom find out in this story?
(E) ☐ a. Any car or truck could be used to try to kill him.
   ☐ b. It would be better for Tom if Trask looked for a new job.
   ☐ c. The men at the body shop did not know how to control the tow truck.
   ☐ d. The police thought that the driver of the blue van was the killer.

Skills Used to Answer Questions

A. Recognizing Words in Context   B. Recalling Facts
C. Keeping Events in Order   D. Making Inferences
E. Understanding Main Ideas

3. Language Skills

Hearing Syllables

Sometimes you have to sound out a long word. It can be hard to do. It will be hard if you try to look at all of the word at the same time. You need to cut up a long word into small parts. These parts are called syllables.

Some words have only one syllable. Look at these words. Say the words to yourself. Hear the one sound.

Tom   ran   stopped   hear

Some words have two syllables or two sounds. Say these words to yourself. Hear the two parts.

police   murder   started   running

Some words have three syllables. Say these words to yourself. Hear the three parts.

radio   policeman   suddenly   anything

Some words have four, or five, or even more syllables. These are very long words that we do not see very much.

It does not matter how many parts or syllables a word has. The parts are always small. Even if there are more of them, you still read them one at a time.

Exercise 1

Here are some words from the story. Copy them. Write them on the line next to each word. Say each word as you write it. Hear the parts. Write the number of syllables on the last line. The first one has been done.

1. thinking _*thinking*_ _2_

2. quietly _____ _____

3. looked _____ _____

4. somewhere _____ _____

5. walked _____ _____

6. around _____ _____

7. himself _____ _____

8. started _____ _____

9. happened _____ _____

10. boxes _____ _____

Finding Syllables

What if you do not know a word? Can you still tell how many syllables it has? Yes. You just need to know what a syllable looks like.

1. Every syllable must have a vowel. There may be more than one vowel, but if there is no vowel in a part of a word, the part is not a syllable. These parts are syllables. Underline the vowels.

can	un	o	peer

These parts are not syllables. There is no vowel.

str	pl	ng	ss

2. Every syllable has one vowel sound. The syllable may have more than one vowel, but you only hear one sound. You do not hear the second vowel. Or the two vowels make one sound. Say these words to yourself. Hear the one sound. Underline all of the vowels.

hear	cook	street	nice

With some words you can see the syllables right away. Say these words to yourself. Hear the two syllables.

into	upset	himself	breakfast

Each of these words is really two small words made into one big word. Look at the words again. See that each syllable is a small word. Underline each small word.

in-to	up-set	him-self	break-fast

When you see a word that is made up of two small words, you know that each small word is a syllable. You can split the big word between the two small words.

Exercise 2

These words from the story are made up of two small words. Show the two small words by printing them on the lines. The first one has been done for you.

1. somewhere   _SOME_ / _WHERE_

2. downstairs   _____ / _____

3. highway   _____ / _____

4. itself   _____ / _____

5. maybe   _____ / _____

6. outside   _____ / _____

7. someone   _____ / _____

8. myself   _____ / _____

9. upstairs   _____ / _____

10. something   _____ / _____

3. Understanding Life Skills

Highway Directions

The big highways we use today are known by many names. They are called *expressways, turnpikes, interstate highways,* and *superhighways.*

Cars can go fast on highways because there are no cross-roads, traffic lights or people walking. Because cars go so fast on highways, drivers must think fast if they do not want to get into an accident. Because of the high speeds, you must think ahead. You must try to expect what could happen. And you must act right away.

Highway Rules. Here are some of the rules you are expected to follow when you drive on the highways. Use what you have learned about reading directions. in Chapter 1 and Chapter 2 to help you read these directions. Answer the Chapter questions with each rule.

1. You may get sleepy if you have to drive for a long time. Once each hour, pull off the road and rest.

On which one of these trips should you plan rest stops? Put an *x* in the right box.

☐ a. An all-day trip to another state
☐ b. A daily ride to work and back home
☐ c. A trip to the market for shopping

2. On the highway, stay in the right lane until you get up to speed. Don't break into traffic when you are going slowly.

At which one of these speeds is it all right to break into traffic? Circle your answer.

10 MPH   25 MPH   50 MPH

3. When you want to pass, look for cars coming fast behind you. Use the turn signal before pulling out to pass, and use the turn signal again before turning back in.

If a car has just passed you and you see the turn signal go on, what can you expect? Put an x in the right box.

- ☐ a. The car is going to pull back into the lane in front of you.
- ☐ b. The car is going to pull over and stop.
- ☐ c. The car wants to slow down and get back in lane behind you.

4. If your car breaks down, get off the road and lift your front hood.

Why should you lift the hood? Put an x in the right box.

- ☐ a. Lifting the hood is a signal that you need help.
- ☐ b. There is something wrong with your motor.
- ☐ c. The spare tire is under the front hood.

5. Leave lots of space between you and the car in front of you. Leave a space of one car for every ten miles of speed.

How many car spaces should you leave if you are going 50 miles per hour? Circle your answer.

5   10   50

Try to be careful when you are driving on the highway. There are not as many accidents on today's high speed roads, but the accidents that do happen are bad ones.

3. Applying Life Skills

Reading Traffic Signs

When you drive, you have to look at signs on the road. You have to do what the signs tell you to do. Good drivers will be sure to look at signs because they know that the signs are put up to help them.

Traffic Signs. Look at the traffic signs below. Read the directions that go with each one. Then answer the questions.

A STOP sign means that you must bring your car to a full stop. Slowing down is not good enough. STOP signs always have eight sides.

1. Why do STOP signs always have eight sides? Put an *x* in the right box.

□ a. A sign with only six sides would not look right.

□ b. The special shape helps drivers see them quickly.

□ c. The word STOP will not fit on a four-sided sign.

A YIELD sign means that you must give way to cars coming from other roads. A YIELD sign works like a STOP sign, except that you do not have to come to a full stop unless another car is coming.

2. What is the shape of a YIELD sign? Draw a line under your answer.

Circle   Square   Triangle

A WRONG WAY sign is used at the off ramp of big highways. These signs keep a driver from using an off ramp as an on ramp by mistake.

3. What should you do if you see a WRONG WAY sign in front of you? Put an *x* in the right box.

☐ a. Get out of your car right away and leave it where it is.

☐ b. Keep going ahead and hope that no one sees you.

☐ c. Stop your car, look around, and back up to get off the ramp right away.

The numbers on SPEED signs tell you the fastest speed that is safe. You can go this speed if the weather and daylight are all right. If it is raining or snowing, if the road is slippery, or if it is dark, you must go at a slower speed.

4. Look at the 4 lines below. *Three* of them tell about times when you should go *slower* than the SPEED signs say. Put an *x* in those 3 boxes.

☐ a. On a sunny day   ☐ c. During an ice storm

☐ b. On a rainy night   ☐ d. When men are fixing the road

Other signs like this one tell you about things you should not do. These are signs with a picture or arrow on them. The line across the sign means not to do something. The words under the sign tell you what the sign means. This sign means that you should not ride a bicycle on this road.

5. Below are more signs like the bicycle sign. To the side are the words that go with the signs. Draw lines to join the signs to their words. The first one has been done for you.

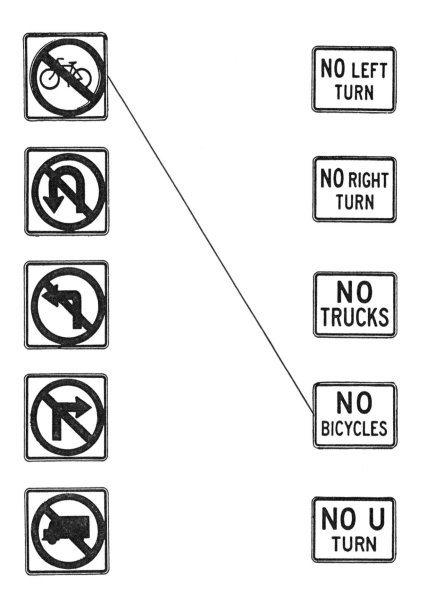

4. Preview Words

Study the words in the box. Then read the sentences below with your teacher. Look carefully at the words with lines under them.

ahead	closely	keys	scratch
anywhere	driveway	outrun	short
backwards	dropped	poison	smiled
bedroom	everyone	roadblock	upset
bushes	joy	roared	write

1. I do not feel safe anywhere.
2. The policeman dropped him off and drove away.
3. I just get so upset.
4. The cook smiled at Tom.
5. The lab said that it was a very hard poison to find.
6. Maybe I should write a note to the police.
7. He landed on the bushes and rolled to the ground.
8. Tom grabbed the keys and jumped into the car.
9. The motor roared as the Rolls went faster and faster.
10. "Maybe I can outrun them," he thought.
11. A car was parked in a driveway.
12. Just then the car shot backwards out of the driveway.
13. I have to get out of town before everyone gets killed.
14. The other car stopped short.
15. Now he could see something in the road ahead.
16. There were lots of police cars. It was a roadblock!
17. Trask walked all around the car, looking at it closely.
18. Not a scratch on it!" Trask said.
19. A joy ride! Who was Trask trying to fool?
20. My bedroom is right next door to the den.

4. Poisoned!

CHAPTER TEN

The policeman took Tom to the police station. Tom told the police what had happened at the auto body shop. He told them about the tow truck going after him. The policeman told the others about the blue van.

They started to check for the blue van. One policeman asked Tom, "Do you want to go home?"

"Yes, I might as well go home," Tom said. "I do not feel safe there. But I do not feel safe anywhere."

"You will be all right," the policeman said. "We think that Trask is OK."

"Well, I do not have a radio in my room. If they want to get me, they will have to think of something new. By the way, have you checked out my uncle's death again?"

"The lab should be calling very soon. We will give you a call as soon as we hear."

"Thank you. Well, we might as well go."

So Tom went home. The policeman dropped him off and drove away. When Tom went into the house, the cook was waiting for him.

"The police again!" she said. "Is everything all right?"

"Yes, everything is all right," Tom said. "They just gave me a ride home."

"Oh. I just get so upset. Sometimes I just do not know what to do," the cook said.

"There, there," Tom said, smiling down at her. "I will take care of you." He thought about what the policeman had asked him. It was funny to think of this poor, scared old woman in on his uncle's murder.

"Oh, Mr. Ladd, I am glad that you are home. It makes me feel so much better," the cook said.

"Good."

"Now, let me get you some supper," the cook said.

"OK," Tom said. "That would be nice. I will go wash up."

Tom went upstairs and washed up. He started to feel better. It was good to be home after all.

He went downstairs. The table was set. The cook was bringing in the food. It looked good.

The cook smiled at Tom. "Sit down, Mr. Ladd," she said, "I like to see a man eat well."

Tom sat down. He started to eat.

"Do you like it?" the cook asked.

"Oh, yes," Tom said. "It is very good."

"I am so glad you like it. I made it just for you. Now, can I get you something to drink?"

"Yes, that would be nice," Tom said. He went on eating.

Just then the phone rang. The cook picked it up. "Mr. Ladd," she called, "it is for you."

"Thank you," Tom said. He went to the phone. "This is Tom Ladd," he said.

"Hello, Mr. Ladd. I am calling from the police station. I am very glad you are home. We have some big news for you."

"You do? What is it?" Tom asked.

"As you know, we had the lab check into your uncle's death again," the man said. "We just got a call from them. They said that you were right. Your uncle was murdered."

"He was? How? Do they know how?" Tom asked.

"Yes. The lab said that he was poisoned."

"Poisoned!" Tom almost shouted. Then he turned quickly to see if the cook could hear him. "Poisoned!" he said again, very quietly. "How was it done?"

"The lab said that it was a very hard poison to find. That is why it took them so long to call us. They said that it must have been in his food. Or it could have been in a drink. This kind of poison takes a long time to act. He could have eaten it at supper and not died till later."

"Oh," Tom said.

"Mr. Ladd, are you all right?" the policeman asked.

"I hope I am. Oh, how I hope I am," Tom said. "Tell me one more thing. If they had found out that my uncle had been poisoned before he died, could they have saved him?"

"No, I do not think so," the policeman said. "Not with the kind of poison that was used. When you take it, that is that."

"Thank you," Tom said quietly.

"Is there anything we can do for you?" the policeman asked. "You sound funny."

"Not right now," Tom said. "But stay by the phone. I might need you later . . . fast."

"OK. Good-bye."

"Good-bye," Tom said. Suddenly that was a sad thing to say.

Tom sat down at the table again. He looked at the food. He had eaten a lot of it. Was it poisoned? When would he find out?

He started to think about what he had told the cook. He had told her everything! He had told her everything he knew. The car . . . the radio . . . the tooth . . . everything! What a fool he had been. It was a good thing he had not eaten at home much. But what good was that now?

But maybe it was not the cook. Maybe Trask had put something in his uncle's food. Maybe . . .

But Trask never went near the food. And Tom started to think about all the times he had talked to the cook. She was always asking him things. She was always waiting for him when he came in. She always knew when he went out. "Then she called the blue van," he said to himself.

"What did you say?" the cook asked as she came in with his drink.

"Oh, nothing," Tom said. "I was just talking to myself."

"Oh. Well, here is your drink. Now, do you want anything more?"

"No," Tom said. "I am so tired. I could not sleep last night. I think I will go to bed."

"Oh, you poor thing," the cook said. "But you should eat your food. I know how upset you are. But you have to eat, you know."

"I know," Tom said. "I will take it upstairs with me and eat it later."

He went to his room and sat down on his bed. He sat and looked at the floor. "I have to think!" he said to himself. "I have to think! I may not have much more time."

CHAPTER ELEVEN

Tom looked at the plate of food. He looked at the drink. "Maybe I should write a note to the police," he thought. "Then they will know who poisoned me if I . . . if I . . ." He put his head in his hands.

"No, that will not work," he thought. "If the cook has poisoned me, she will come up here soon. She will come up to check on me. Then she will see the note and take it away."

Tom got up and walked around his room. "How do you know if you have been poisoned?" he asked himself. "What does it feel like? What . . .

"Now stop that!" he told himself. He sat down again. "I have to think! What should I do? The first thing is to let the police know what has happened. Or what may have happened. Then, if I die, they will pick up the cook."

Very quietly, he went into the next room. He picked up the upstairs phone to call the police. But there was something funny going on. Then he knew. Someone was using the downstairs phone. It had to be the cook! Maybe she was calling the blue van!

Tom waited. He was very, very quiet. He could hear the phone ringing at the other end. Then someone picked it up.

"This is Ann," the cook said. "I think he is on to me!"

"He knows? How?" a man asked.

Tom thought, "I know that man! Who is it?"

"I made him some food," the cook was saying. "He was eating it. Then he got a phone call. After that, he would not eat."

"Where is he now?" the man asked.

"Who is it? Who is that man?" Tom asked himself.

"He is upstairs," the cook said. "He said he wanted to sleep."

"No one goes to bed at supper time!" the man said. "Well, we will have to come and get him. No more of this fooling around. It is time to put an end to it. He knows too much. We will have to get him quickly before he gets away."

"All right. I will watch him till you get here," the cook said.

"You do that," the man said. "If you let him get away now . . ."

"That will not happen." The cook hung up.

Tom hung up, too. There was no time to call the police! He had to get out!

He went quietly to the window. It was a long way to the ground. But there were some bushes under him. That would help. He would have to risk it.

He did not stop to think any more. He opened the window and jumped.

He landed on the bushes and rolled to the ground. He hurt all over, but he got up and ran. Keeping low, he ran to the Rolls.

What luck! Trask was there, working on the car. Tom ran up and hit him over the head. Trask landed hard, nearly out cold. Tom grabbed the keys and jumped into the car.

Tom pulled out into the street. The Rolls was so big! Could he drive it, after his little MG? He had to.

He checked for a radio, but he could not find one. His uncle was too smart for that.

He drove down the street. By now, Trask was up again. Tom could see him come running out into the street, waving his arms. "Well, Trask," he thought, "you will just have to wait for the blue van."

The blue van! There it was, coming at him down the street! How did it get there so fast?

Quickly, Tom turned into a side street. He stepped on the gas. The motor roared as the Rolls went faster and faster. Tom was starting to get the feel of the big car.

He looked back. The blue van was just turning into the side street. It was moving fast, too.

Tom turned again and again, trying to shake them off. But every time he looked back, the blue van was there.

"Maybe I can outrun them," he thought. He turned onto a big street. He stepped on the gas, and the Rolls moved out. He looked back. The blue van was getting smaller. He was getting away!

Tom felt good. He liked the feel of the big motor. "If I have to die," he thought, "this is a good way to do it."

A car was stopped in a side street. Suddenly, it roared out at him. Tom could see the driver's face. The man was scared nearly to death. He was out of control!

His radio! Yes, the other car had a radio. Tom turned fast, and the other car roared by him. It went up on the sidewalk and stopped.

But now another car was coming at him! This driver looked scared, too. Tom missed him. But then another was coming. Tom could see the driver pulling and pulling at the wheel. Tom drove up on the sidewalk to get around him. Then he was back in the street again, moving faster than ever. They had missed him again. But how much longer could he keep it up?

CHAPTER TWELVE

Tom looked down the street. Soon he would be downtown. There would be too many cars. He could not get around them all.

Tom drove down a side street. There were no cars on the street, but soon the blue van was in back of him. He would have to get out of town. That would be the best way.

A car was parked in a driveway. The hood was up, and someone was working on the motor. "If that motor is running . . ." Tom thought. He stepped on the gas so as to get by quickly.

Just then the car shot backwards out of the driveway. It just missed the Rolls and ran up on the grass on the other side of the street. The man who had been working on it ran after it. He was shouting and waving his arms. He almost ran in front of the blue van.

"I have to get out of town," Tom thought, "before *everyone* gets killed."

He turned and turned again, trying to pick streets with no cars on them. At last he was on the highway.

There were still lots of cars. Tom watched for cars with radios. The car in front of him had one. Yes, the car suddenly slowed down. Tom had to turn quickly to miss it.

Now a car from the other side of the highway was coming at him. The driver's face showed how scared he was. Tom stepped on the gas and suddenly turned and went around in back of the other car. The other car stopped short with a screeching of brakes, but Tom was around him. He could see the driver sitting in the car with his face in his hands.

Tom drove on. But now he could see something in the road ahead. As he got closer, he could see that it was a police car. No, it was lots of police cars. It was a roadblock!

Tom drove up to the roadblock as fast as he could go. Then he stepped on the brakes fast. He dove out of the Rolls and ran to the police cars.

The blue van had stopped down the road. It was quickly turning around. Most of the police pulled out to go after the van.

"Turn off your radios!" Tom shouted after them. "Turn off your radios! Turn off your radios or they can control your cars!"

Now the first police car was close to the blue van. Suddenly the police car went off the road. The next police car stopped suddenly, and the car in back of it had to go off the road to keep from hitting it.

Tom ran to one of the cars that was still in the roadblock. "Tell them to turn off their radios!" he shouted to the policeman in the car. "The blue van has something in it that can control a car by radio waves!"

"That sounds crazy!" the policeman said.

"I know it sounds crazy!" Tom said. "But look at them! They are all over the place! The blue van can control them!"

The policeman looked. "Maybe you are right," he said. He turned on his radio. "Calling all cars," he said. "Calling all cars. Turn off . . ." Suddenly his car started up and drove off the road. The policeman fell to the floor. The car drove up the side of the road till it hit a tree.

Tom ran up to the next car. "Tell them . . ." he started to say.

But the policeman was ahead of him. "Calling all . . ." was as far as he got. His car pulled out and drove away on the other side of the road.

There was one more car. As Tom was running to it, a man jumped out of the back seat. The policeman in the front seat was trying to call for help. Suddenly his car started up. It drove off the road backwards, with the policeman hanging onto the wheel.

Tom was alone with the man who had jumped out of the police car. He turned to look at the man.

It was Trask.

CHAPTER THIRTEEN

Tom backed up slowly. Could he get to the Rolls first? "Hello, Trask," he said.

"Mr. Ladd!" said Trask. "Was that *you* who took the Rolls?"

"Yes, it was," Tom said. When was Trask going to make his move?

"Gee, Mr. Ladd. You did not have to hit me," Trask said. "You can have the keys to the car any time you want. After all, it is your car now."

Tom did not know what to say. Then he jumped to one side as Trask walked quickly to the Rolls. Trask walked all around the car, looking at it closely.

"Not a scratch on it!" Trask said. "Not bad! I saw the way you were driving it. I thought it would be all scratched up."

Tom watched Trask. What was going on? What did he care about the car?

Then Trask looked at him. Suddenly Tom could see that Trask was scared of him, too.

"Mr. Ladd . . ." Trask said.

"What?"

"Mr. Ladd, why were you driving like that? You just do not seem like the kind of man who would hit his uncle's driver over the head and take his uncle's car for a joy ride."

A joy ride! Who was Trask trying to fool?

"Well," said Tom, "I am glad that you care about something, even if you do not care about my uncle or me. I am glad that you care about the Rolls. But if you did not want me to drive it like that, you should have called off your friends in the blue van."

"Not care about your uncle? My friends in the blue van? What are you talking about?" asked Trask.

"*You* know," Tom said. But then he looked at Trask's face. He did not look mean. He just looked upset. Maybe he did *not* know!

"What about the night my uncle was killed?" Tom asked. "How did you get to his den so fast when the cook screamed?"

"My bedroom is right next door to the den," Trask said. "I woke up fast and I moved fast. What would you have done?"

"What about the tooth?" Tom asked. "You told the police that it had been gone for a long time."

"It had," Trask said. "Then he got a new one. But he did not keep the new one in there all the time."

Trask looked at Tom. "Why are you asking me all this?" he asked. "See here, Mr. Ladd. I worked for your uncle for a long time. I liked him a lot. When he died, I was very upset to think that his work would be stopped. I did not know what he was working on, but I knew that it was big. Your uncle was a smart man. Like I said, I liked him a lot. I *did* care about him."

Trask stopped. Tom looked at him and saw that he was almost crying. Maybe Trask was not in on it after all.

"How did you get here?" Tom asked. "Why were you in the police car?"

"The police came right after you left," Trask said. "They said that you had sounded funny on the phone, so they wanted to check up on you. I told them that someone had taken the Rolls. So they took me with them."

"Did they go in the house?" Tom asked.

"Yes, they went in looking for you," Trask said. "The cook said that you were upstairs sleeping. But when they went to look for you, you were gone."

"So the cook will be gone, too," Tom said to himself.

"So they came back out, picked me up, and we came here," Trask said. "You know, now that I think of it, I did see that blue van you were talking about. I saw it right after you took off in the Rolls. And I saw it again just now. That is who the police were after! Who is in the van?"

"The same people who killed my uncle," Tom said. Then, before Trask could say anything, he said, "We should get out of here."

"Yes, Mr. Ladd," Trask said. "Um . . . do you want me to drive?"

Tom could see that Trask really wanted to drive. Was it just that he was scared of the way Tom was driving? Or was he really one of the killers?

"He looked as if he really cared about my uncle," Tom thought. "But did he? His story was good. But was it just a story? Look at that cook! She could cry and look upset any time she needed to! Do I really want to be in a car with that man?"

Just then a police car drove up. "Well, I got back on the road at last," the policeman said. "You must have been right about that radio, Mr. Ladd. We should see if we can find that van. Do you want to ride with me?"

"OK," Tom said. "I will ride with him. You take the Rolls," he told Trask.

That took care of that. He did not have to drive with Trask. But who cared? If he was full of poison, he still did not have long to live.

4. Comprehension Questions

Directions. Answer these questions about the story you have just read. Put an *x* in the box beside the best answer to each question.

1. What is the main thing that Tom finds out in this story?
(E) ☐ a. His uncle was poisoned.
    ☐ b. It was a hard poison to find.
    ☐ c. His uncle may have poisoned himself.
    ☐ d. Tom was poisoned by the cook.

2. What did the lab say about the poison?
(B) ☐ a. It took a long time to kill.
    ☐ b. It would kill someone right away.
    ☐ c. It could be stopped if it was found in time.
    ☐ d. It was not strong. It would not kill anyone.

3. When Tom found out about the poison, he felt like a fool
(C) for talking to the cook. When he would tell her things about the case, what would happen next? She would
    ☐ a. become scared of being poisoned, too.
    ☐ b. become scared that the police would think she did it.
    ☐ c. tell the other killers what he knew about them.
    ☐ d. tell the killers that he knew who they were.

4. The cook called the killers. How did Tom find out?
(B) ☐ a. He made her tell him.
    ☐ b. He picked up the phone.
    ☐ c. The police told him.
    ☐ d. Trask told him.

5. What happened soon after Tom hit Trask over the head?

(C) ☐ a. Tom found out that he might have been poisoned.

☐ b. The cook called her friends in the blue van.

☐ c. Tom opened a window and jumped to the ground.

☐ d. Trask told the police that someone had taken the Rolls.

6. Why did Tom drive the Rolls out of town?

(D) ☐ a. This was the best way to get the killers all mixed up.

☐ b. He wanted to lead the killers away from his uncle's house.

☐ c. He knew there was a police roadblock on the highway.

☐ d. There would not be as many cars for the killers to control.

7. Tom could see the driver of the car he had nearly hit. The

(A) driver was sitting in the car with his <u>face in his hands</u>. This means that the driver felt

☐ a. sleepy.

☐ b. scared.

☐ c. mad.

☐ d. sick.

8. Tom said, "You should have <u>called off</u> your friends."

(A) What do you do when you call off your friends?

☐ a. Tell them to stop.

☐ b. Call out loud to them.

☐ c. Call them on the phone.

☐ d. Tell them where to get off.

9. Why did the cook run away?

(D) □ a. Trask was going to kill her.

□ b. Tom knew that she was the killer.

□ c. The men in the blue van were after her.

□ d. She was sorry for what she had done.

10. At the end of the story, how does Tom feel about Trask?

(E) □ a. He is sure that Trask is the killer.

□ b. He is sure that Trask knows who the killers are.

□ c. He does not think that Trask is a killer, but he is not sure.

□ d. He knows for sure that Trask is not one of the killers.

Skills Used to Answer Questions

A. Recognizing Words in Context   B. Recalling Facts

C. Keeping Events in Order   D. Making Inferences

E. Understanding Main Ideas

Breaking Words into Syllables

Some big words are made up of two small words. But most big words are not. How can you tell where one syllable stops and the next one starts? How can you tell how to break the word into syllables?

There are ways of telling where to break the word. These ways use patterns of vowels and consonants.

Here are the patterns for breaking words.

Pattern 5: V — C/C — V. If there are *two* consonants between two vowels, break the word *between* the consonants.

Break these pattern 5 words. First say the word to hear how many syllables it has. Write the syllables on the lines next to each word. The first one has been done for you.

chapter ___*chap*___ / ___*ter*___

after _____ / _____

letter _____ / _____

running _____ / _____

Say these words again to yourself. Do you hear the vowel sound in each syllable? Remember, every syllable must have a vowel sound.

Pattern 6: V/C—V. If there is *one* consonant between two vowels, break the word *before* the consonant.

Break these pattern 6 words. First say the word to hear how many syllables it has. Print the syllables on the lines next to each word. The first one has been done for you.

police   _____*PO*_____ / _*LICE*_____

open   _____ / _____

motor   _____ / _____

before   _____ / _____

Say the words again to yourself. Listen for the vowel sound in each syllable.

Exercise 1

Break these words into syllables. Write the syllables on the lines next to each word. On the last line tell if the word fits pattern 5 or pattern 6. The first one has been done for you.

1. better *bet* / *ter* 5

2. doctor _____ / _____ ___

3. murder _____ / _____ ___

4. paper _____ / _____ ___

5. propel _____ / _____ ___

6. supper _____ / _____ ___

7. under _____ / _____ ___

8. remain _____ / _____ ___

9. sadly _____ / _____ ___

10. broken _____ / _____ ___

Words with Many Syllables. What if a word has more than two syllables? You just use the same two patterns again. You can use them again and again till you come to the end of the word.

To break a long word, use these three steps:
1. Look for pattern 5 or 6.
2. Break at the syllable.
3. See if the syllable has a vowel sound.

Then go back to step 1 to find the next syllable. Let's use these three steps with this long word: **entertainment.**

Step 1: Look for 2 consonants between 2 vowels or look for 1 consonant between 2 vowels.

e n t e r t a i n m e n t
↑ ↑ ↑ ↑
(V C C V)

Step 2: Break at the syllable.

e n / t e r t a i n m e n t

Step 3: See if there is a vowel sound in the syllable.

e n
↑
(VOWEL SOUND)

Go back to step 1 to find the next syllable.

Step 1: Look for 2 consonants between 2 vowels or look for 1 consonant between 2 vowels.

e n / t e r t a i n m e n t
       ↑ ↑ ↑ ↑
     (V C C V)

Step 2: Break at the syllable.

e n / t e r / t a i n m e n t

Step 3: See if there is a vowel sound in the syllable.

t e r
  ↑
 (VOWEL SOUND)

Go back to step 1 to find the next syllable.

Step 1: Look for 2 consonants between 2 vowels or look for 1 consonant between 2 vowels.

e n / t e r / t a i n m e n t
                ↑ ↑ ↑ ↑
              (V C C V)

```
Step 2:    Break at the syllable.

           e  n / t  e  r / t  a  i  n / m  e  n  t
```

```
Step 3:    See if there is a vowel sound in the syllable.

                        t  a  i  n
```

```
                     (VOWEL SOUND)
```

Go back to step 1 to find the next syllable.

```
Step 1:    Look for 2 consonants between 2 vowels or
           look for 1 consonant between 2 vowels.

           e  n / t  e  r / t  a  i  n / m  e  n  t

   This last part does not fit pattern 5 or 6. Is it the last
syllable in the word? It is a syllable if it has a vowel
sound.

                        m  e  n  t
                        ↑
                     (VOWEL SOUND)
```

Hear is the word with all its syllables:

           e n / t e r / t a i n / m e n t

Let us look at another long word and break it into syllables, using the steps: superhuman.

Use the steps and find the first syllable. **Print it on** the lines below:

_ _ /_____

Use the steps and find the next syllable. **Print it** below:

_ _ /_ _ _ /_____

Use the steps and find the third syllable. **Print it** below:

_ _ /_ _ _ /_ _ /_____

Is the last part a syllable? It is a syllable if it has a vowel sound and does not fit patterns 5 or 6. **Print all of** the syllables below:

_ _ /_ _ _ /_ _ /_ _ _

It should look like this:

SU/PER/HU/MAN

Exercise 2

Break these words into syllables. **Print** the syllables on the lines next to each word. The first one has been done for you.

1. suddenly   _SUD_ / _DEN_ / _LY_

2. important   _____ / _____ / _____

3. republican   ____ / ____ / ____ / ____

4. forgetful   _____ / _____ / _____

5. vitamin   _____ / _____ / _____

6. wonderful   _____ / _____ / _____

7. happiness   _____ / _____ / _____

8. consonant   _____ / _____ / _____

9. innocent   _____ / _____ / _____

10. compensation   ____ / ____ / ____ / ____

4. Understanding Life Skills

"How To" Directions

One of the many kinds of things you have to read almost every day is directions. Directions tell you how to do something. You find directions in many places — in books, on boxes and cans, on papers and forms, and so on.

If you want to do or make something, you have to read the directions. What is the best way to do this?

Let's look at some directions you might have to read and follow:

How to Make Coffee

Step 1. Fill a clean coffee pot with cold, fresh water.

Step 2. Measure coffee into basket placed on stem. Use 2 tablespoons of coffee for each three-quarters of a measuring cup of water. Place stem in pot.

Step 3. Percolate coffee for 10 minutes over medium heat. Begin timing when water turns color.

Step 4. When coffee is ready, remove basket with grounds and replace cover.

Step 5. Serve coffee at once or keep hot over low heat. Do not boil.

Suggestion: Once you open a new can of coffee, try to use it up within a week. If coffee has gone stale, do not use it.

Let's see the best way to read these directions. Answer the questions. Print your answers.

1. Read carefully. Look at every word. Do not skip anything. How many steps are given in these directions?

_____

2. Look at each step. Try to see what you have to do in each step. Look at everything in one step before going on to the next. What is the last thing you should do in step 2 before going on to step 3?

_____ _____ _____ _____

3. Read all of the directions first. Do not start to work right away. Read everything in the directions before you do anything. Something said at the end might be important for you to know before you begin. For example, your can of coffee might be old. What does the suggestion at the end tell you not to do with stale coffee?

_____ _____ _____ _____

4. Read the directions again. It is always a good idea to read directions twice. Be sure before you start that you have read everything you need to know.

5. Look at the pictures. See if there are any pictures. These can help a lot. They can help you see what you have to do. Are there any pictures with these directions?

_____

6. Do the directions step by step. Do everything in step 1 before going on to step 2. Just think about the step you are on. If you are on step 3, when should you begin timing?

_____ _____ _____ _____

7. Check your work. Check to see if you have done everything the directions said to do. See if everything has been done right. If there is a picture, see if your work looks like the picture.

What is the last thing you are told to do in step 5?

_____ _____ _____

It may take a long time to read all of the directions. You have to take the time. If you do not do what the directions say, what you are doing will not come out right. You may even put yourself in danger.

4. Applying Life Skills

Following "How To" Directions

Here are the directions for fixing a faucet that is leaking. Read the directions. Then answer the questions. Use what you have just learned about following "how to" directions to help you. Print your answers using block letters.

How to Repair a Leaky Faucet

1. Turn off the water. Look under the sink for a valve or faucet on the pipe going up to the sink.

2. Wrap white tape around the packing nut so that you will not scratch it when you loosen it. See the picture to find the packing nut.

3. Loosen the packing nut carefully. Lift out the faucet and stem. You may have to turn it to lift it out.

4. Remove the screw at the bottom of the stem. Take out the old washer. Clean the place where the washer was.

5. Put in a new washer that fits. Put the flat side of the washer in first. Put the screw back in.

6. Clean the valve seat and put the faucet and stem back in. Carefully tighten the packing nut.

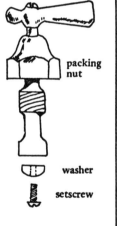

Stem Assembly

Caution: Test the faucet before removing the white tape. If water leaks around the packing nut, give the nut another turn or two.

Questions

Answer these questions based on the directions you have just read. **Print** your answers on the lines following each question.

1. What three parts of the stem are named in the picture?

a. _____

b. _____

c. _____

2. What is the name given for everything shown in the picture?

_____

3. What is the first thing you are told to do in step 1?

_____

4. What is the last thing you are told to do in step 6?

_____

_____

5. When should you read the caution which comes after step 6? Draw a line under the right answer.

a. Before you begin any steps

b. After you have done step 6

c. If the faucet still leaks

6. Write the number of the step which tells you how to put the new washer in.

_____

7. Copy the sentence which tells you what you may have to do if the faucet and stem does not lift out.

_____

_____

8. Steps 3 and 6 tell you how to loosen and tighten the packing nut. What word is used to tell you how to handle the packing nut?

_____

9. If the packing nut is scratched, which step was not done right?

_____

10. Copy the sentence which tells you what to do after you remove the screw at the bottom of the stem.

_____

_____

5. Preview Words

Study the words in the box. Then read the sentences below with your teacher. Look carefully at the words with lines under them.

airport	cards	hospital	seaplane
apart	careful	leaned	sleepy
arrest	danger	loudspeaker	sped
boomed	held	propeller	swung
bottom	helicopter	rights	yourselves

1. The police car <u>sped</u> back into town.
2. He gave them a set of big <u>cards</u> and a big black pen.
3. <u>Danger</u>! Bad radio waves are being sent out.
4. Soon a police car came by with a <u>loudspeaker</u> on top.
5. A <u>helicopter</u> came down out of the sky.
6. "Are you all in place?" the loudspeaker <u>boomed</u>.
7. Give <u>yourselves</u> up! We are all around you!
8. It was a small <u>seaplane</u>.
9. The <u>propeller</u> went around and around.
10. The other man <u>held</u> up his hand.
11. We will put that plane at the <u>bottom</u> of the river.
12. He looked <u>sleepy</u>.
13. He <u>leaned</u> out of the window and held up the card.
14. The other man <u>swung</u> at him.
15. We have to get this man to a <u>hospital</u>!
16. I will tell you on the way to the <u>airport</u>.
17. We will find it if we have to take that house <u>apart</u>.
18. Now be quiet, and I will read you your <u>rights</u>.
19. You are under <u>arrest</u> for the murder of Ned Ladd.
20. He wanted to be so <u>careful</u>.

5. Who Was It?

CHAPTER FOURTEEN

The police car sped back into town. The Rolls was right in back of it.

Suddenly another police car pulled up next to them. The two cars pulled over to the side of the road. The Rolls waited down the street. The driver of the other car jumped out and ran up to them. He had something in his hands.

"We know what part of town the blue van is in," the policeman said quickly. "Bill tracked them. He had been working with Ladd, here, so he knew about the radio. He turned off his radio and tracked them down by the river."

"OK," said the driver of the car that Tom was in. "Now what?"

"We will move in soon," the first policeman said. "No radios. Use these." He gave them a set of big cards and a big black pen. "We have roadblocks set up. We will move in at 8:00."

"OK. We will be there."

They drove on down the street with the Rolls in back of them. "I wish Trask would go home," Tom thought. "He still scares me a little."

Suddenly another police car sped by. The big card was up in the window. "MAIN & RIVER STREET," it said.

They turned down Main Street. They could see other police cars moving in from other streets.

One car was stopped by the side of the street. The motor was not running. The policeman in the car was talking on his radio.

As they drove by, they could hear what he was saying. "All CB people . . . this is the police. Danger! Take your ears off! Turn off your radios! Danger! Bad radio waves are being sent out. They can crack up your car. All CB people, shut it on down!"

Soon a police car came by with a loudspeaker on top. "Turn off all radios! Danger! Turn off all radios!" the loudspeaker shouted.

"They think of everything!" Tom thought. "But can they find the blue van again? Do they know how small the control is? They will never find that!"

Now a helicopter came down out of the sky. It hung in the air over them. It tipped a little, and they could see a big card in the window. It said, "BLUE VAN 2 STREETS DOWN." They waved their hands, and the helicopter roared away.

They turned down River Street. More and more police cars were coming. The helicopter roared over them.

There was the blue van!

Was there anyone in it?

The helicopter roared down and tipped. "STAY BACK. MAY HAVE GUNS TOO," the card said.

All the cars stopped. Policemen started to get out. The car with the loudspeaker pulled up. "Are you all in place?" the loudspeaker boomed.

All the policemen waved. Their guns were out. They looked at the blue van.

"You in the blue van!" the loudspeaker shouted. "Give yourselves up! We are all around you! Give yourselves up! Come out now!"

They waited.

Nothing happened.

"Come out now with your hands up!" the loudspeaker boomed again.

Nothing happened.

The police started to move closer. The helicopter came in closer. All Tom could hear was the roar it made.

Suddenly Tom could hear another roar. He looked up. It was a small seaplane. It was flying right at the helicopter.

The helicopter had to drop quickly and then take off away from the plane. The plane turned and landed hard on the river. The motor was still going, and the propeller went around and around.

Tom could see the man in the plane. He was hanging over the back of the seat. Was he dead or just out cold?

Now the policemen grabbed their guns. The door of the van had opened.

A man got out. Then another.

They stood by the van. The first man shouted, "Do not move, any of you."

The other man held up his hand. "We have the control. We are going to get in that plane. Do not try to stop us. If you try to stop us, we will put that plane, and the man in it, at the bottom of the river."

The two men moved to the plane. The policemen stood still, watching them.

Suddenly Tom saw that the man in the plane had come to. He was sitting up. He was looking at all the police cars. He looked sleepy, but . . .

He had to try. Tom grabbed the big black pen and a card. "TURN OFF MOTOR. TURN OFF RADIO," he wrote.

He leaned out of the window and held up the card. The man looked away. Tom waved the card and shouted. The man looked at him. He looked at the card. Could he see it from that far away?

The seaplane's propellers stopped turning.

The men from the van turned and looked at the plane. They ran to it, shouting. The loudspeaker boomed, "Stop!"

Suddenly someone was running at the two men. It was Trask! He jumped on the man who had held up his hand. The other man swung at him. All three went down.

Policemen started to run up to them. Tom jumped out of the car and ran, too.

Trask had grabbed one of the men. He was fighting hard. His face looked almost crazy.

Trask grabbed something away from the man. He jumped to his feet and pulled back his arm. He had something in his hand.

The other man grabbed his gun. He hit Trask on the back of the head.

But just as he was hit, Trask's arm went out. The tiny thing went flying out of his hand. As everyone watched, it went out ... out ... over the river. Then down ... and it was gone.

And Trask fell down on his face like a tree.

CHAPTER FIFTEEN

The police were all around the men from the van. They took their guns and started to take them to the cars.

Tom came running up. "Wait!" he said. "There is another man!"

"Who?" the police asked.

"I do not know. But the man on the phone did not sound like these men." Tom told the police about the call that the cook had made. "I know who it is. But I just can not think of it," he said.

"Well, we can take these men in," a policeman said.

"And we have to get this man to a hospital!" called another policeman. Trask was still out cold.

"Yes, we have to move fast. Just tell us if you think of it," the first policeman said.

So the two men were taken to the police station. Trask was rushed to the hospital. Tom and three police cars sped to the house to pick up the cook.

She was gone.

Tom ran upstairs to his room. He looked for the food and drink.

It was gone, too.

"She will not have gone very far," said one of the policemen. He gave Tom a pat on the back. "We will find her."

"I know. But I wish that she had left that food."

"What food?" the policeman asked.

Tom told him about the food he was eating when he got the phone call. "The lab told me that my uncle had been poisoned," he said. "And there I was eating supper. I had eaten a lot of it."

"How do you feel?" the policeman asked.

"All right," Tom said "But I keep waiting to fall over. How long before I know?"

"I do not know. But if she has taken the food, we can not ask the lab. We will have to ask her."

"How?" Tom asked. "She is gone."

"We will put up roadblocks everywhere," the policeman said. "She will not get away."

They ran out to the car. "I can use my radio now," the policeman said. "But it still feels funny to turn it on."

He turned on the radio. "Calling all cars," he said. "Pick up Mr. Ladd's cook for murder one. She is about five feet tall. She is about 60 years old. She may have a gun. Check the train station and the airport. Check all cars going out of town. Over."

"Let me know if you find her," Tom said. "I am going to go to the hospital. I want to see Trask. And it will be a good place to be if I fall over."

"OK. But keep thinking about that man on the phone," the policeman said.

"I will," Tom said.

Trask was still out cold. Tom sat and looked out the window. He tried to think about other things. But all he could think about was Trask . . . and himself. Would they make it?

At last Trask woke up. "Mr. Ladd!" he said. "Where am I?"

"In the hospital," Tom said. "One of the men from the blue van hit you."

"Oh, yes," Trask said. "The blue van ... the radio control ..."

"It was very brave of you to jump on the men," Tom said.

"Well, I could not stand to see your uncle's work used like that," Trask said. "He wanted to help people. But when bad people got the control ... It is better for it to be at the bottom of the river!"

"I think you are right," Tom said. "I want to thank you for helping me. It was good of you, after the way I hit you."

"Oh, that is all right. After all, Mr. Ladd was your uncle. He would have wanted me to help you."

"He must have been a good man," Tom said.

"Yes, he was. Everyone cared about him."

"Not everyone," Tom said.

"What did you say?" Trask asked.

"Oh, nothing," Tom said.

"Not everyone cared about him? Is that what you said?"

"Now, now, I just ..." Tom felt bad. He did not want to upset Trask.

"Well, you are right, in a way," Trask said. "Everyone but Mr. Day."

"Mr. Day!" Tom shouted.

"Yes. After that fight, he said he did not care. But I think he still did. I ..."

"Mr. Day! Yes! That is it! Where is the phone?" Tom asked.

"Mr. Ladd, what is going on? What are you talking about?" Trask asked.

Just then a policeman ran in. "Mr. Ladd, can you come to the airport?" he asked. "We think we have her. But we need you to tell us."

"Who? Who do you have?" Trask asked.

"No one," Tom said. "You just rest." Trask did not need to know yet what the cook had done to his uncle. "But I know who was on the phone!" Tom told the policeman. "I will tell you on the way to the airport."

When he got to the airport, he saw why the police had called for him. It was the cook, all right, but she did not look the same. She did not look old or upset any more. She looked mad. She was saying, "I do not know what you are talking about! Now let me get on my plane!"

Then she saw Tom. Suddenly she looked old and upset again. "Oh, Mr. Ladd," she said. "I am so glad you are here! I do not know what is happening. These men have me so scared!"

Tom looked at her. He almost felt like saying, "There, there." But all he said was, "Yes, that is the cook."

"I have not done anything!" the cook shouted. "You do not have anything on me."

"We will find it if we have to take that house apart," one policeman said.

"And I think that you are an old friend of ours," another policeman said. "When we get you back to the station, I think that we will find that we have a lot of other things we can pin on you, too. We have been waiting for you for a long time. Now be quiet, and I will read you your rights."

Then they sped to Mr. Day's house. It was very near Tom's house. "That is how the blue van got there so fast," Tom told the police.

When they got to the door, Mr. Day was there. It was as if he were waiting for them.

"Mr. Day," a policeman said, "you are under arrest for the murder of Ned Ladd."

"Yes, yes. I know. I will not run. I just want to get it over with." He looked as if he were going to cry. "That control was mine, too. At any rate, I helped him think of it.

"But he wanted to make it so safe. He wanted to be so careful that no one could use it in a bad way. I told him that he would never get it done that way. So we had a fight. And I told him that I would get it away from him. But he hid it. So when his old cook left, I got a woman to get the job as his new cook. She found out where he hid the control. So we got those two men . . ."

"Mr. Day!" the policeman said. "You have the right . . ."

"Yes, yes. I know. I do not have to say anything. But I want to get it over with. Quickly. I told the two men just to get the tooth. I did not tell them to kill him. How was I to know that the woman was going to poison him? Poor Ned!

"And he was right, you know. That control had to be made safe. Look what those two men have done with it! Why did I ever let them have it? What was I thinking of? I just want it all to be over!"

"It *is* all over now, Mr. Day," Tom said quietly.

Tom went home. He felt tired. Everything was done. His uncle's funeral would be the next day. Tom hoped that Trask would be well so that he could go.

It was dark out. It was very late. "So I must be all right," he thought. "The food must not have been poisoned. What about the drink? Was the drink poisoned? Did the police call me just in time? I will never know."

Tom went into his uncle's den and sat down. He looked around at the books and papers. "Poor Uncle Ned," he thought. "It is all over now. Your work is gone. It did not change the world."

Tom thought about it. "And I have to say one thing. I am glad that it did not."

5. Comprehension Questions

Directions. Answer these questions about the story you have just read. Put an *x* in the box beside the best answer to each question.

1. The policeman turned off his radio and <u>tracked</u> the killers.
(A) This means he
 ☐ a. stayed right behind them.
 ☐ b. tied them to a train track.
 ☐ c. went with them in the van.
 ☐ d. trapped them near the tracks.

2. The policeman tracked the blue van to
(B) ☐ a. the roadblock.
 ☐ b. the airport.
 ☐ c. the river.
 ☐ d. Tom's house.

3. The loudspeaker shouted, "Give yourselves up! We are all
(C) around you!" What were the killers in the van doing?
 ☐ a. Taking over a small seaplane
 ☐ b. Turning down River Street
 ☐ c. Trying to get away from Trask
 ☐ d. Just waiting

4. While the police were looking for the cook, Tom went
(C) ☐ a. after the blue van.
 ☐ b. to the hospital to see Trask.
 ☐ c. to Mr. Day's house.
 ☐ d. to the airport to help them look.

5. Trask asks Tom and the policeman, "Who? Who do you
(D) have?" Tom does not tell Trask that the cook had
poisoned his uncle. Why not?
   □ a. He still thinks Trask might be in on it.
   □ b. He thinks that she might have poisoned Trask, too.
   □ c. The doctor told him that Trask could not talk to
   anyone.
   □ d. He does not want to upset Trask while he is sick.

6. One policeman says to the cook, "I think that you are
(A) an old friend of ours." He means that
   □ a. he has met her before.
   □ b. she used to work at the police station many years
   back.
   □ c. he thinks she is a nice woman.
   □ d. the police had been after her before for other crimes.

7. Mr. Day did not run from the police. Why not?
(D) □ a. He knew that the cook would tell the police about
   him.
   □ b. He knew that Tom would tell the police where he
   was.
   □ c. He did not feel that he had done anything bad.
   □ d. He felt bad about everything that had happened.

8. Why did Mr. Day have a fight with Ned Ladd?
(B) □ a. Ladd wanted to use the control to take over the
   world.
   □ b. He thought that Ladd was being too slow and
   careful.
   □ c. Mr. Day wanted to keep the control all for himself.
   □ d. Ladd hid the control where Mr. Day could not find it.

9. Mr. Day had told the cook and the two men
(E) ☐ a. to kill Ned Ladd and get the control.
   ☐ b. to get the control back but not to kill Ned Ladd.
   ☐ c. to help Ned Ladd to make the control work.
   ☐ d. to get the control and throw it in the river.

10. After Ned Ladd's death, what happened to his work with
(E) cars and radio waves?
   ☐ a. Tom took over his uncle's work.
   ☐ b. Mr. Day said that he would make the control safe.
   ☐ c. No one would ever use the control again.
   ☐ d. Tom planned to look for the control in the river.

Skills Used to Answer Questions
A. Recognizing Words in Context   B. Recalling Facts
C. Keeping Events in Order   D. Making Inferences
E. Understanding Main Ideas

---

5. Language Skills

Vowel Sounds in Long Words

Vowel and consonant patterns help us to break words into syllables. As we saw in Story 2 patterns also tell us if vowel sounds are long or short. This does not always work for every word, but it does give us a good start.

Let us look again at the patterns from Story 2.

Pattern 1: C—V. This pattern has a vowel at the end with one or two consonants in front. The vowel at the end is long. Words like she and go fit this pattern.

This pattern also works for syllables. The a in pa/per is long because the first syllable fits the C—V pattern.

Break these words into syllables to show the pattern of the first syllable. **Print** the syllables on the line next to each word. The first one has been done for you.

paper   _____PA_____ / ____PER____

below   _____ / _____

motor   _____ / _____

propeller   _____ / _____ / _____

Look at the first syllable in these words. It follows the C—V pattern. Hear the long vowel.

Pattern 2: C−V−V−C. This pattern has two vowels together between consonants. The first vowel is long. You do not hear the second vowel. Words like soap and chain fit this pattern.

This pattern also works for syllables. The a in com/plaint is long because the second syllable fits the C−V−V−C pattern.

Break these words to show the syllable which fits pattern 2. It may be the first syllable or the second syllable. Print the syllables on the lines next to each word. The first one has been done for you.

complaint *COM* / *PLAINT*

reveal _____ / _____

maintain _____ / _____

roadblock _____ / _____

Look at each syllable which has the C−V−V−C pattern. The first vowel is long. You do not hear the second vowel.

Pattern 3: C−V−C−V. This pattern has a consonant and a vowel and then another consonant and a vowel. In this pattern the first vowel is long. The last vowel is an **e**, and you do not hear it. Words like **broke** and **time** fit this pattern.

This pattern also works for syllables. The **a** in **safe/ty** is long because the first syllable fits this pattern.

Break these words to show the syllable which fits pattern **3**. Print the syllables on the lines next to each word. The first one has been done for you.

safety   _____*SAFE*_____ / _____*TY*_____

beside   _____ /_____

excitement _____ /_____ /_____

lately   _____ /_____

   Look at each syllable which fits the C−V−V−C pattern. Hear the long vowel. See the other vowel you do not hear.

Pattern 4: C—V—C or V—C. This pattern tells you that the vowel is short. If there is only one vowel and there are one or more than one consonants before or after it, the vowel is short. Words like spill and ask fit this pattern.

This pattern also works for syllables. The two vowels in sud/den are short because both syllables fit this pattern.

Break these words to show the syllables which fit pattern 4. **Print** the syllables on the lines next to each word. The first one has been done for you.

sudden   _____SUD_____ / _____DEN_____

happen   _____ / _____

upset   _____ / _____

investment _____ / _____ / _____

Look at the words again. Hear the short vowels. They are short because all of these syllables fit the C—V—C or V—C pattern.

Exercise

Break these words into syllables. **Print the syllables on the lines next to each word.**

Then, above each syllable, tell if the vowel sound in each syllable is long (L) or short (S). The first two have been done for you.

                      S   L   S

1. mistreatment   MIS / TREAT / MENT

                   L   S

2. frozen   FRO / ZEN

3. custom   _____ / _____

4. unbutton   _____ / _____ / _____

5. funny   _____ / _____

6. attack   _____ / _____

7. sadly   _____ / _____

8. himself   _____ / _____

9. biggest   _____ / _____

10. condiment   _____ / _____ / _____

11. grateful   _____ / _____

12. gunman   _____ / _____

13. hopefully   _____ / _____ / _____

14. innocent   _____ / _____ / _____

15. refinement   _____ / _____ / _____

16. painless   _____ / _____

17. pavement   _____ / _____

18. plentiful _____ /_____ /_____

19. priceless _____ /_____

20. retirement _____ /_____ /_____

5. Understanding Life Skills

Directions on Labels

We all have to read the labels that come with drugs and medicines. These kinds of labels have to be read very carefully for two reasons. One, we want to take the right amount of the drug so that we can get better. Two, we do not want to use the drug in the wrong way.

Here is what to look for on a medicine label:

1. What it is for
2. What it is *not* for
3. How to take it
4. What to watch out for
5. How to keep it

You may not always find all five of these things on a label, but you should always look for them.

Let us look at a label. This comes from the label on a well-known headache medicine. We have put the numbers in to help you find the five things to look for.

EXTRA-STRENGTH TYLENOL

Extra Pain Relief
Contains No Aspirin
50 Capsules — 500 mg. each

(1) INDICATIONS
For the temporary relief of minor aches, pains, headaches and fever.

(3) USUAL DOSAGE
Adults: Two capsules three or four times daily. No more than a total of eight capsules in any 24-hour period.

(2) Severe or recurrent pain or high or continued fever may be indicative of serious illness. Under these conditions, consult a physician.

(4) WARNING: Keep this and all medication out of the reach of children. In case of accidental overdose, contact a physician immediately.

Let us see how this label covers the five things we should look for. Answer the questions. Print your answers.

1. What it is for. See number 1 on the label. If you have a headache, or an ache, or a pain, or a fever that is minor (not too bad), this medicine will help for a while. Which word means "for a while"?

_____

2. What it is not for. See number 2 on the label. Do not use this medicine for a severe (bad) pain, or for a pain that keeps coming back. Which word means "keeps coming back"?

_____

Do not take this medicine for a high fever or for a fever that stays. Which word tells about a "fever that stays"?

_____

If you have these things, you may be very sick. You should see a doctor. Which three words mean "see a doctor"?

_____

3. How to take. See number 3 on the label. Adults (people who are grown up) should take 2 of these. You may take the capsules 3 or 4 times a day. What is the most you should take in a day?

_____

The label does not say how many capsules children should take. Should you give this medicine to a child?

_____

4. What to watch out for. See number 4 on the label. There is a warning, or something to be careful about. You should keep this medicine and all medicines away from children. What is another word for "medicine"?

If you take too much by accident, you should see a doctor right away. Which two words mean "take too much by accident"?

Which word means "right away"?

---

5. How to keep. This medicine does not say how it should be kept. Sometimes a label will tell you to keep the medicine in a dry place, or not to keep it in a hot place.

There are other things this label tells you.

This *Tylenol* is stronger than usual. Which two words say this?

——

How many capsules are there in this jar?

When you read labels on drugs or medicines, look for the five things we have talked about. Be sure you find number 4, the things to watch out for. All medicines can make you sick if you do not take them in the right way.

5. Applying Life Skills

Reading Directions on Labels

Here are the five things to look for on medicine or drug labels.

1. What it is for

2. What it is not for

3. How to take it

4. What to watch out for

5. How to keep it

The next page shows the directions found on *Alka-Seltzer Plus*, a medicine for colds. Read the directions carefully once. Then read these questions. Look back at the directions to find the answers. Print your answers on the lines.

Questions

1. How many tablets are in this box?

_____

2. Some people do not like to take medicine that tastes bad. Which three words tell you that this medicine does not taste bad?

_____

_____   _____

FAST, EFFECTIVE RELIEF OF THE SYMPTOMS OF HEAD COLDS, SINUS CONGESTION AND HAY FEVER.

The tablets contain:

A DECONGESTANT—helps restore free breathing, shrink swollen nasal tissue and relieve sinus congestion due to head colds or hay fever.

AN ANTIHISTAMINE—helps relieve the runny nose, sneezing, sniffles, itchy watering eyes that accompany colds or hay fever.

SPECIALLY BUFFERED ASPIRIN—relieves headache, scratchy sore throat, general body aches and the feverish feeling of a cold.

SEE NEW LABEL

Alka-Seltzer® Plus Cold Medicine

Effective Relief from Major Cold Symptoms

FAST, EFFECTIVE RELIEF GUARANTEED

Refreshing Lemony Flavor

36 TABLETS

RECOMMENDED DOSAGE: Adults: Take 2 tablets dissolved in water every 4 hours, not to exceed 8 tablets daily. Children (6–12): ½ adult dosage. Children under 6 years: Consult your physician.

CAUTION: Individuals with high blood pressure, diabetes, heart or thyroid disease should use only as directed by physician. If drowsiness occurs, do not drive a car or operate machinery.

NOTE: Occasionally a trace amount of moisture may cause a slight effervescence within the foil pouch causing the pouch to puff slightly. This does not alter the quality of the product.

STORE AWAY FROM HEAT.

3. These tablets have three kinds of medicine: a decongestant, an antihistamine and buffered aspirin. Each medicine does a different job. Here are all the things that these tablets are good for.

Put **D** in front of the jobs that the decongestant does.

Put **A** in front of those things that the antihistamine helps.

Put **BA** in front of the ones which show what the buffered aspirin is good for.

The first one is done to help you get started.

_____A_____ a. Makes a runny nose better.

_____ b. Helps your headache feel better.

_____ c. Helps to stop sneezing.

_____ d. Makes breathing easier.

_____ e. Makes your sore throat feel better.

_____ f. Helps free a blocked nose.

_____ g. Helps your fever go away.

_____ h. Helps your eyes stop watering.

_____ i. Makes your body aches go away.

_____ j. Helps you to stop sniffling.

4. a. How many tablets should adults take at one time?

_____

   b. What is the most adults should take in a day?

_____

5. a. How many tablets should a 10-year-old girl take at one time?

_____

   b. What is the most she should take in one day?

_____

6. How often should someone take this medicine?

_____

7. Who can tell you if you should give this medicine to your 5-year-old boy? (Put an x in one box.)
   □ a. Your doctor   □ c. Your husband or wife
   □ b. Your druggist   □ d. Your mother

8. People with these 4 kinds of sickness should not take this medicine unless their doctor tells them to. (Put an x in all the right boxes.)
   □ a. Thyroid disease   □ d. Heart disease
   □ b. Bad eyesight   □ e. Stomach cramps
   □ c. High blood pressure   □ f. Diabetes

9. What should you not do if this medicine makes you sleepy? (Put an *x* in the right boxes.)
   - ☐ a. Do not go to work.
   - ☐ b. Do not drive your car.
   - ☐ c. Do not take a nap.
   - ☐ d. Do not run a chain saw.

10. Keep this medicine away from one of these places. (Put an *x* in the right box.)
   - ☐ a. A refrigerator
   - ☐ b. A stove
   - ☐ c. A window

TO THE INSTRUCTOR

To the Instructor

Purpose of the Series

Teachers charged with the responsibility of providing instruction for adults and older students with reading difficulties face a major problem: the lack of suitable materials. Stories written at the appropriate level of maturity are too difficult; stories easy enough to read independently are too childish.

The stories in the Adult Learner Series were written to solve the readability problem. The plots and characters in these stories are suitable for adults and older students, yet the stories can be read easily by very low-level readers.

The principal goal of the series is to provide interest and enjoyment for these readers. To this end, every attempt has been made to create a pleasant reading experience and to avoid frustration. The plots move quickly but are kept simple; a few characters are introduced and developed slowly; the same characters are utilized throughout a text; sentence structure and vocabulary are carefully monitored.

A secondary goal is to help adults explore and develop everyday life skills. Lessons and exercises about a variety of life skills provide adults and older students with the basic competencies they need for success in this fast-paced world.

Rounding out the structure of the series are exercises for developing vocabulary skills, comprehension skills, and language skills.

Reading Level

The stories in the Adult Learner Series are all written at second grade reading level. It should be kept in mind, however, that the stories were written for adults: people with a wider range of experience and larger speaking and listening vocabularies than those of elementary school children. Thus, there are some words and some events which might present difficulties for elementary school students but which should not pose problems for older beginning readers.

Besides the slightly increased complexity of vocabulary and plot, the writing style itself has been adapted for older beginning readers. Every effort was made to make the prose sound natural while maintaining simplicity of structure and vocabulary. The repetition of words and phrases has been carefully controlled to permit maximum learning of new words without producing a childish effect.

The reading level of the stories was established by the use of the *Fry Readability Formula* and the *Dale-Chall List of 3,000 Familiar Words*. According to the Fry formula, the range of reading levels in the series is from grade 1.2 to 2.4. Ninety percent of the words used are from the Dale-Chall list.

Structure and Use of the Text

Each book in the Adult Learner Series is divided into several units. Each unit follows a regular format consisting of these sections:

Preview Words. Twenty words from each story are presented for students to preview before reading. The words are listed first in alphabetical order and then shown again in story sequence in sentences relating to the story.

The twenty sentences match the story in readability; students can read the sentences independently. With some classes the instructor may want to read the words and sentences aloud for students to repeat and learn. In very structured classes, the words could also be used for spelling and writing practice.

Story. The primary purpose of the story is to provide interesting material for adult readers. It should be read as a story; the element of pleasure should be present. Because of the second grade reading level, students should be able to read the story on their own.

The pages containing stories are marked throughout the text. Students should be encouraged to return to these pages often and re-read the stories.

Comprehension Questions. Ten multiple-choice comprehension questions follow each story. There are two questions for each of these five comprehension skills:

        A. Recognizing Words in Context
        B. Recalling Facts
        C. Keeping Events in Order
        D. Making Inferences
        E. Understanding Main Ideas

The letters *A* through *E* appear in the text as labels to identify the questions.

Students should answer the questions immediately after reading the story and correct their answers using the key at the back of the book. Students should circle incorrect responses and check off the correct ones.

The graphs at the back of the book help the instructor keep track of each student's comprehension progress. The *Comprehension Progress Graph* shows comprehension percentage scores. The *Skills Profile Graph* identifies areas of comprehension weakness needing special attention and extra practice.

Language Skills. These sections cover many aspects of language study: phonics, word attack skills, simple grammar, and correct usage. The readability of these sections is higher than that of the stories. The readability level varies depending on the vocabulary load of the specific language skill being taught.

Because the language skills are taught in clear and simple terms, most students will be able to work these sections independently. However, the instructor should be alert for opportunities to explain and further illustrate the content of the lessons.

The lessons contain exercises which give students the opportunity to practice the language skills being taught. An answer key at the back of the book makes it possible for students to correct their work.

Understanding Life Skills. Every story is accompanied by two sections which deal with life skills. The first, "Understanding Life Skills," introduces and fully explains a specific life skill. The life skills all revolve around some detail of modern adult life.

Because this section stresses *understanding* a certain life skill, the reading level is higher than the reading level of the story. However, the life skill lessons are presented in carefully prepared steps, and most students should be able to read and comprehend them without too much difficulty.

Questions used in the lessons are designed to focus the students' attention and to reinforce the learning. Answers for all questions are provided at the back of the book.

Applying Life Skills. Because modern-day living requires both *knowing* and *doing*, two life skills sections follow each story to emphasize both aspects. The second, "Applying Life Skills," is primarily a practical exercise.

This section builds on the understanding generated in the previous section. Students should be able to complete the exercise successfully by applying what they have just read.

Completing this section allows students to demonstrate their mastery of a specific life skill. It gives them the first-hand experience they need with tasks they are likely to encounter in everyday living.

An Answer Key at the back of the book helps students correct their work and gives them immediate feedback.

All units in each book are structured alike, each consisting of the six sections described here. Students quickly discover the regular pattern and are able to work with success and confidence throughout the text.

Summary of the Stories in *Murder by Radio*

Story 1: What Happened? (Level 1.2) Tom Ladd's Uncle Ned, an inventor, is found dead. The police assume a heart attack, but Tom suspects murder. He sets out to find out what his uncle was working on.

Story 2: Someone Wants to Kill Me! (Level 1.5) Tom finds out about his uncle's invention, a device to control vehicles through their radios. The invention is small enough to be concealed in a tooth. When he goes for a drive, Tom's car is mysteriously taken over and caused to crash.

Story 3: The Radio (Level 1.4) Two more attempts are made on Tom's life: a delivery truck chases him into a house, and a tow truck picks him up on its hook. A blue van is spotted at the scene.

Story 4: Poisoned! (Level 1.5) Tom finds out that his uncle had been poisoned and realizes that the cook may have just poisoned him as well. He escapes from the house, only to meet his uncle's chauffeur, Trask, whom he also suspects.

Story 5: Who Was It? (Level 1.6) The police track the blue van without the use of radios. The killers almost escape in a seaplane, but Tom foils them. The cook is apprehended, and Tom figures out that his uncle's former colleague is behind the murder.

Because *Murder by Radio* is the first book of the Adult Learner Series and thus designed for the very beginning reader, there may be need for more teacher involvement during the reading of the story than with the other books of the series. The instructor should look for opportunities to discuss with the students the events of the story as they occur.

Students should be made aware of the genre of the murder mystery and its special literary conventions. Readers will gain far more enjoyment and understanding of the story if the instructor urges them to sift the clues as they become available and try new solutions to the mystery as they progress through the stories.

ANSWER KEY

Answer Key
Comprehension Questions

Story 1

1. c	2. b	3. a	4. a	5. d
6. d	7. d	8. b	9. c	10. b

Story 2

1. a	2. b	3. c	4. c	5. d
6. a	7. a	8. d	9. c	10. d

Story 3

1. b	2. d	3. b	4. a	5. c
6. d	7. d	8. c	9. c	10. a

Story 4

1. a	2. a	3. c	4. b	5. d
6. d	7. b	8. a	9. b	10. c

Story 5

1. a	2. c	3. a	4. b	5. d
6. d	7. d	8. b	9. b	10. c

Answer Key
Language Skills

Story 1
Exercise 1

1. on   *n*   *o*   S

2. ran   *r, n*   *a*   S

3. know   *k, n, w*   *o*   L

4. by   *b*   *y*   L

5. still   *s, t, l, l*   *i*   S

6. night   *n, g, h, t*   *i*   L

7. cup   *c, p*   *u*   S

8. no   *n*   *o*   L

9. next   *n, x, t*   *e*   S

10. Tom   *T, m*   *o*   S

Story 1
Exercise 2

1. most   M, S, T   O   L

2. tell   T, L, L   E   S

3. kind   K, N, D   I   L

4. last	L,S,T	A	S
5. at	T	A	S
6. fight	F,G,H,T	I	L
7. best	B,S,T	E	S
8. so	S	O	L
9. sky	S,K	Y	L
10. shut	S,H,T	U	S

Story 2
Exercise

1. got	GOT	4	S
2. cake	CAKE	3	L
3. but	BUT	4	S
4. cup	CUP	4	S
5. thank	THANK	4	S
6. next	NEXT	4	S
7. note	NOTE	3	L

8. suit	SUIT	2	L
9. nice	NICE	3	L
10. stop	STOP	4	S
11. boat	BOAT	2	L
12. if	IF	4	S
13. left	LEFT	4	S
14. no	NO	1	L
15. fell	FELL	4	S
16. stone	STONE	3	L
17. made	MADE	3	L
18. top	TOP	4	S
19. big	BIG	4	S
20. mean	MEAN	2	L

Story 3
Exercise 1

1. thinking   *thinking*   2

2. quietly   *quietly*   3

3. looked   *looked*   1

4. somewhere   *somewhere*   2

5. walked   *walked*   1

6. around   *around*   2

7. himself   *himself*   2

8. started   *started*   2

9. happened   *happened*   2

10. boxes   *boxes*   2

Story 3

Exercise 2

1. somewhere _____SOME_____ / _WHERE_

2. downstairs _____DOWN_____ / _STAIRS_

3. highway _____HIGH_____ / _WAY_

4. itself _____IT_____ / _SELF_

5. maybe _____MAY_____ / _BE_

6. outside _____OUT_____ / _SIDE_

7. someone _____SOME_____ / _ONE_

8. myself _____MY_____ / _SELF_

9. upstairs _____UP_____ / _STAIRS_

10. something _____SOME_____ / _THING_

Story 4
Exercise 1

1. better ___*bet*___ / ___*ter*___ 5

2. doctor ___*doc*___ / ___*tor*___ 5

3. murder ___*mur*___ / ___*der*___ 5

4. paper ___*pa*___ / ___*per*___ 6

5. propel ___*pro*___ / ___*pel*___ 6

6. supper ___*sup*___ / ___*per*___ 5

7. under ___*un*___ / ___*der*___ 5

8. remain ___*re*___ / ___*main*___ 6

9. sadly ___*sad*___ / ___*ly*___ 5

10. broken ___*bro*___ / ___*ken*___ 6

Story 4

Exercise 2

1. suddenly   SUD / DEN / LY

2. important   IM / POR / TANT

3. republican   RE / PUB / LI / CAN

4. forgetful   FOR / GET / FUL

5. vitamin   VI / TA / MIN

6. wonderful   WON / DER / FUL

7. happiness   HAP / PI / NESS

8. consonant   CON / SO / NANT

9. innocent   IN / NO / CENT

10. compensation   COM / PEN / SA / TION

Story 5

Exercise

1. mistreatment   <u>MIS</u> / <u>TREAT</u> / <u>MENT</u>
              S   L   S

2. frozen   <u>FRO</u> / <u>ZEN</u>
        L   S

3. custom   <u>CUS</u> / <u>TOM</u>
        S   S

4. unbutton   <u>UN</u> / <u>BUT</u> / <u>TON</u>
        S   S   S

5. funny   <u>FUN</u> / <u>NY</u>
        S   S

6. attack   <u>AT</u> / <u>TACK</u>
        S   S

7. sadly   <u>SAD</u> / <u>LY</u>
        S   S

8. himself   <u>HIM</u> / <u>SELF</u>
        S   S

9. biggest   <u>BIG</u> / <u>GEST</u>
        S   S

10. condiment   S   S   S
CON / _DI_ / _MENT_

11. grateful   L   S
GRATE / _FUL_

12. gunman   S   S
GUN / _MAN_

13. hopefully   L   S   S
HOPE / _FUL_ / _LY_

14. innocent   S   S   S
_IN_ / _NO_ / _CENT_

15. refinement   L   L   S
_RE_ / _FINE_ / _MENT_

16. painless   L   S
PAIN / _LESS_

17. pavement   L   S
PAVE / _MENT_

18. plentiful   S   S   S
PLEN / _TI_ / _FUL_

19. priceless   PRICE /LESS

20. retirement   RE / TIRE /MENT

Answer Key
Understanding Life Skills

Story 1

1. _NO_   6. _NO_

2. _NO_   7. _YES_

3. _YES_   8. _YES_

4. _YES_   9. _NO_

5. _NO_   10. _YES_

Story 2

1. _TOLL_ _FREE_

2. _DIAL_

3. _COD_

4. _4TH_ _CLASS_ _MAIL_

5. $ _1.75_

Story 3

1. a   2. 50 MPH   3. a   4. a   5. 5

Story 4

1. 5
2. PLACE STEM IN POT
3. DO NOT USE IT

5. NO
6. WHEN WATER TURNS COLOR
7. DO NOT BOIL

Story 5

1. TEMPORARY
2. RECURRENT
   CONTINUED
   CONSULT A PHYSICIAN
3. EIGHT
   NO
4. MEDICATION
   ACCIDENTAL OVERDOSE
   IMMEDIATELY
5. EXTRA – STRENGTH
   50

Answer Key
Applying Life Skills

Story 1

1. | MAY |

2. <u>Put</u> a line under the first word in this sentence.

3. <u>Murder by Radio</u>

4. ○ ○ ○ ○ ○ ○ ○ ○ ○

5. <u>Always / read / and / follow / directions / carefully.</u>

6. Tom said, "I think my uncle was murdered."

7. ⑩ (40)

8. _____ PRINT _____

9. <u>Trask, drive me home, please.</u>

10. and 11.

| A | E | I | O | U |

12.

 □    ☒    □

13.

14. X̶ 2 X̶ 4 X̶ 6 X̶ 8 X̶ 10 X̶1 12 X̶3 14 X̶5

15. *SOMEONE WANTS TO KILL ME!*

Story 2

1. a   6. No

2. No   7. No

3. 25 Pounds   8. b

4. Yes   9. a

5. c   10. b

Story 3

1. b   2. Triangle   3. c   4. b, c, d

5.

Story 4

1. a. _____ PACKING NUT _____

   b. _____ WASHER _____

   c. _____ SETSCREW _____

2. _____ STEM ASSEMBLY _____

3. _____ TURN OFF THE WATER. _____

4. _____ CLEAN THE PLACE _____
_____ WHERE THE WASHER WAS. _____

5. a. Before you begin any steps

6. _____ 5 _____

7. _____ YOU MAY HAVE TO TURN _____
_____ IT TO LIFT IT OUT. _____

8. _____ CAREFULLY _____

9. _____ STEP 2 _____

10. _____ TAKE OUT THE OLD _____
_____ WASHER. _____

Story 5

1. _____36_____

2. _____REFRESHING_____

_____LEMONY_____   _____FLAVOR_____

3. a. _____A_____   f. _____D_____

b. _____BA_____   g. _____BA_____

c. _____A_____   h. _____A_____

d. _____D_____   i. _____BA_____

e. _____BA_____   j. _____A_____

4. a. _____2_____   b. _____8_____

5. a. _____1_____   b. _____4_____

6. _____EVERY FOUR HOURS_____

7. a   8. a, c, d, f   9. b, d   10. b

COMPREHENSION PROGRESS GRAPH
AND SKILLS PROFILE GRAPH

How to Use the Comprehension Progress Graph

1. At the top of the graph, find the number of the story you have just read.

2. Follow the line down until it crosses the line for the number of questions you got right.

3. Put a dot ● where the lines cross.

4. The numbers on the other side of the graph show your comprehension score.

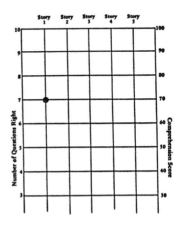

For example, this graph shows the score of a student who answered 7 questions right for Story 1. The score is 70%.

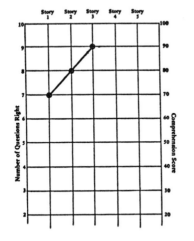

This same student got scores of 80% and 90% on Stories 2 and 3. The line connecting the dots keeps going up. This shows that the student is doing well.

If the line between the dots on your graph does not go up, or if it goes down, see your instructor for help.

Comprehension Progress

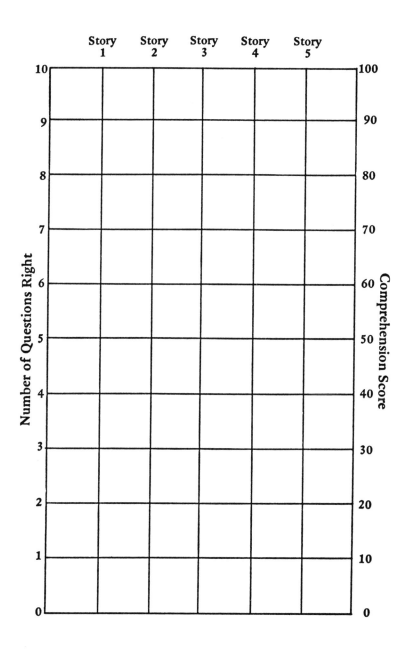

How to Use the Skills Profile Graph

1. There is a block on this graph for every comprehension question in the book.

2. Every time you get a question wrong, fill in a block which has the same letter as the question you got wrong.

For example, if you get an A question wrong, fill in a block in the A row. Use the right row for each letter.

Look at the graph. It shows the profile of a student who got 3 questions wrong. This student got an A question wrong, a C question wrong, and a D question wrong.

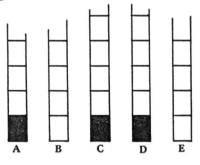

On the next story, this same student got 4 questions wrong and has filled in 4 more blocks.

The graph now looks like this. This student seems to be having trouble on question C. This shows a reading skill that needs to be worked on.

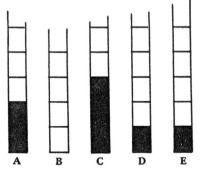

The blocks that are filled in on your graph tell you and your instructor the kinds of questions that give you trouble.

Look for the rows that have the most blocks filled in. These rows will be higher than the others. Talk to your instructor about them. Your instructor may want to give you extra help on these skills.

Skills Profile

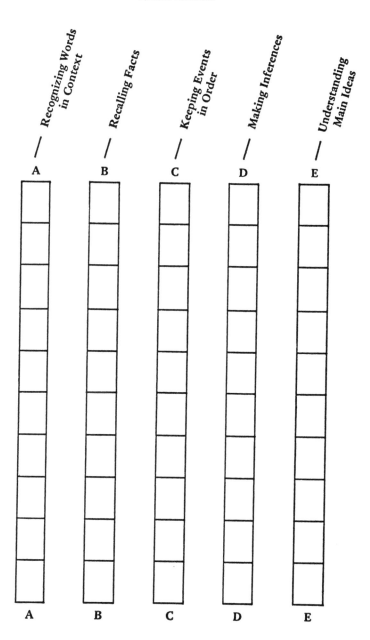